Net Results

The Complete Tennis Handbook

By Rick Devereux

Photographs by the author and
Daniel F. Lyman

A PATHMARK BOOK

Pathfinder Publications, Inc.

Boston

International Standard Book Number 0-913390-07-0
Library of Congress Catalog Card Number 74-80-452
Pathfinder Publications Inc., Boston, Massachusetts

Printed in the United States of America

Contents

CONTENTS

CONTENTS

CONTENTS

Foreword

Rick Devereux, an astute and articulate analyst of the game of tennis, provides in *Net Results* a knowledgeable and well-organized presentation of the game's fundamentals. His experience both as a player and a teacher gives him a penetrating grasp of the essentials of singles and doubles, and he includes many a good trick on how to acquire the necessary technique. This book will be profitable reading for anyone wishing to upgrade his technical and tactical knowledge.

It should be added that *Net Results* is particularly relevant to the average player. It is not one of those "This is how I won Wimbledon and you can too" accounts, rather it is devoted to what the ordinary devotee — as contrasted with the superathlete — can do to improve himself.

Jack Barnaby
Harvard Coach

Introduction

The facts of the "tennis boom" are impressive. Over two years ago the Neilsen ratings put the number of tennis players in the United States in excess of 13 million. That is five times the number of skiers, and the figure was conservatively expected to double within ten years. Some experts say it already has. In the last ten years indoor tennis courts have sprung up around the country the way bowling alleys did in the early sixties. The courts are heated in cold climates or air-conditioned in places where the weather is too warm or rainy. But indoor tennis is only one small manifestation of a boom in a sport which has been enjoyed primarily outdoors for over a hundred years. Weekends, vacations, real estate developments — even lives — center around tennis.

In the past, a certain amount of personal wealth was associated with the game of "lawn tennis" (as the sport was called in England where it began), but today the sport has become popular in urban low-income areas and its popularity is expected to increase, according to all predictions.

As a television spectator sport, tennis is steadily surpassing golf. The special appeals of professional tennis make it unique among popular sports in the United States. For one thing, the many international tennis stars are a highly visible and colorful lot — and they aren't buried beneath helmets and full-length, numbered uniforms. Competing mostly as individuals, tennis players can and do express their personalities, even beyond "gentlemanly" limits. Permission to appeal the umpire's line calls opened the door to a world of emotions.

Sometimes the newly acquired privileges are abused. For instance, during the 1972 finals of the U.S. Open Championships at Forest Hills, the Rumanian, Ilie Nastase, playing against Arthur Ashe, delayed and pouted for nearly ten minutes after being called for foot-faulting early in the first set. The fans, who almost booed Nastase off the court during his delay, ended up cheering him as he later emerged victorious in a dramatic fifth-set reversal. Ashe, who had set the stage for high drama, took his opportunity at the microphone during the match awards to dress down his victor for not "playing tennis." Meanwhile Nastase, winner's check in hand, lolled on the hood of the winner's auto and mused aloud about starting a used-car dealership in Rumania. He had received worse dressing-downs in the past from those less tolerant of his *prima donna* mentality. In fact, he had recently defaulted a match — out of "fear" — when Clark ("Superman") Graebner offered to cross the net and straighten him out by force.

Nor are women, despite the beauty they add to the game, reluctant to show emotions on or off the court. While Billie Jean King cooly out-hustled the aging hustler Bobby Riggs, humiliating him in front of a record number of viewers in the most-talked-about sports event of 1973, Billie Jean's ex-doubles partner, Rosie Casals, aggressively tried to proselytize for "women's lob" in the broadcast booth with Howard Cosell. Cosell's experience in taming Muhammed Ali helped him to restrain Rosie from violence, but others have not been so lucky.

But beyond the drama of professional tennis lie the more fundamental and timeless appeals of the game. At the professional level the strength and endurance involved in playing tennis are almost disguised by the apparent ease and grace with which the court is covered and strokes executed. In this respect a tennis match resembles less a football game than a concert where the performance is measured by the product and not the effort. Yet the grace and beauty of a tennis player are dependent on a vast amount of discipline and knowledge. The discipline is up to the player but knowledge can be shared and the following chapters represent an attempt to pass on the benefits of years of both playing and teaching tennis.

It is my hope, of course, that beginners will continue to use this book while they are progressing to higher levels and that intermediates will do likewise in readying themselves for the changes which are demanded for "advanced" tennis. If your commitment to tennis does not extend to advanced levels, I nevertheless hope that reading *Net Results* will give you an idea how challenging, rewarding, and exciting tennis can be at all levels (and between players of different abilities, sexes, and ages).

Tennis is a demanding sport, but stick with it and you will soon be able to enjoy the sport for a "life time."

1

The Basics of Stroke Dynamics

GETTING THE FEEL OF THE RACKET

In his book *Racket Work: The Key to Tennis* Jack Barnaby, former president of the United States Professional Tennis Association, stresses that one must learn to feel the racket the way one would learn to use a new hand. Before trying to play the piano or to pick pockets, it is better to have mastered shooting marbles or opening doors. One's muscles must memorize very simple actions and learn to perform them automatically before the next basic step is attempted.

Performing automatically, however, does not mean never missing, for unlike playing the piano, tennis is an exercise in errors. Although a stroke may be described in terms of its various parts (backswing, follow-through, footwork), and although it is helpful to practice these parts separately whenever possible, beginners must spend most of their time trying to master entire strokes. Under these circumstances, even the natural athlete can imagine himself a slow learner. Amidst poor shots, outright missing, and subsequent chasing after balls, merely getting the feel of the racket can take a lot of hours. Nevertheless, just hitting more balls will speed up the process of getting the feel. It is as important as breaking in a baseball glove.

Off-Court Exercises. You do not need to be on the court or at the backboard to get the feel of a racket in your hand. One of the most useful ways to pass ten minutes while you are waiting for a court is to bounce a ball gently up and down on your racket. At first it will take more space than you might guess. You should do it every day, counting (silently) until you can hit the ball fifty times without missing. Bouncing the ball on the court with a racket is even better, though a little more difficult at first. When you think you're really getting the feel, try keeping the ball in the air, bouncing it on alternate sides of the racket.

Backboard Exercises. The experience of hitting a ball against a wall is indispensable. In the beginning stand within ten feet of your structure and block the ball as many times as you can, again counting — counting is a must for your concentration in all backboard exercises. After you have mastered a number of long rallies, you should move further away from the hitting surface. A beginner with an hour of time for tennis should spend at least half of it at the backboard — the experience is worth ten hours of hitting against another beginner. Once the ball can be blocked with consistency, a short stroke should be employed. Later you can alternate long strokes with shorter, softer swings, and so on. In addition to counting and alternating different strokes (forehands and backhands, hard and soft), aiming the ball at particular spots will carry you quite far.

Volleys for Beginners? If you have never played tennis, you might think it premature to begin playing net before you have grasped the forehand or backhand strokes, but it is as easy as catching a ball or playing Ping-Pong.

Beginning skiers learn faster on short skis because they are easier to control and, similarly, putting a beginning player at net can miniaturize tennis. The ball can be blocked over a net, which is no longer an obstacle, onto a court that is almost hard to miss. The player is free to concentrate on watching the ball hit the racket — a big help in training the eye and getting the feel of the racket. Because it is easy, or can always be made to seem easy by a teacher who positions the pupil's racket and hits or throws the ball gently against it, volleying is an encouraging experience. Since volleying is often associated with an advanced stage of tennis, success here is sweet.

Early exposure to this type of volley decreases the fear that some players have (especially women) of playing at the net. More teaching pros are now starting pupils with the backhand volley and moving them back, almost literally step by step. The process seems to convey a feeling of gradual progress and a mastery of difficulties by degree. A player who starts himself at the base line can play for a long time before feeling that he is any better than the day he started.

STROKE DYNAMICS

Before going on to discuss the individual strokes in detail, the dynamics involved in hitting a ball, with any stroke, should be understood.

Hitting a tennis ball is a combination of catching and throwing done at twice the speed it would take to accomplish either action separately. Beginners cannot realize the extent to which the control of a shot depends on the player *feeling* the ball on the strings of the racket. The ball does not reflect off the strings as a hardball does off a bat. Rather, it rides the strings, sometimes for as much as half a foot. The impact of a relatively soft ball squashing back into pliable racket strings is a phenomenon too fast for the human eye to see, but it is readily viewable on film. (See fig 1 - 1.)

The longer the ball stays on the strings, the more chance there is to feel it, and thus to control it. The basics of each swing are designed to help you keep the ball on the strings for as long as possible.

Footwork. The first thing every beginner is told is to turn sideways to the net before making a ground stroke. Some players who are quite experienced may even wonder why turning sideways is so important. Good shots are made occasionally without any turn at all, but they are executed most often by advanced players who are also capable of magical "racket work" — those who can sacrifice backswing and follow-through, if the occasion demands. However most advanced players will use any time they have to automatically turn sideways. Although beginners confronted with a ball rarely feel they have *any* time, turning sideways is their key to promoting good ground strokes.

A turn sideways to the net gets the body out of the way to allow room for a good backswing, essential to a full stroke. The body is particularly "in the way" of the backhand backswing. The sideways stance also encourages you to *step with your stroke*, which lengthens your swing and puts your weight behind your arm. Your weight thrown into a stroke increases power, balance, and control; and it saves energy.

Even when you do not have time to turn sideways, which you do not have when you are volleying at the net, a step forward is recommended. Turning and stepping are the essential parts of

Figure 1-1

footwork in tennis, and everyone can learn them. Learning how to move your feet so that you *position* yourself in time to turn and step is another matter.

The Follow-Through. Stepping towards the net just before the ball is hit requires practiced timing. At first a pupil may find it distracting to try to time this step. Often it is easier to acquire some *feel* by concentrating on the follow-through. Unfortunately beginners are apt to think of follow-through as something unimportant that takes place after the ball has been hit (and the damage done). A good follow-through is the only sign of a good swing that can be read by the player himself. By watching the follow-through, a player can gauge the effectiveness of his shot. Of course a good swing does not necessarily make a good shot. Some beginners can imitate a perfectly good swing and hit badly. , This may lead them to think they are doing something wrong, when sometimes what they really need most is experience, the feel. This indefinable feel is common to other sports and activities, such as shooting a basketball, catching a ball, karate, and drawing (a picture or a gun). A good follow-through will lengthen your swing and thus increase your time to feel the ball. Detailed instructions on how to follow through will be given in the chapters on each stroke.

Concentration. Holding a long follow-through, the way a golfer does, has a psychological purpose as well as a dynamic one — it fixes concentration on a part of the swing. The beginner must learn to feel his swing even before he can feel the ball, and the swing can be too complicated a motion to be learned as a whole. The job of the pro is to suggest a phrase that will capture the essence of some aspect of stroking that needs attention and will stick in the pupil's mind. It is not always possible to guess what phrase will perform this "magic." Many phrases are perfectly clear, but the mind may forget a phrase before the body has learned it, and vice-versa, or the mind may insist upon remembering more than the body can handle at one time. It is a matter of chance whether or not your mind and body are tuned in to some fortunate combination which will aid your learning tennis.

A good pro can help tune you in by suggesting an amount he thinks you need. As a rule, suggesting too little is safer than too much (the pro who repeats himself over and over is not telling all he knows). My first suggestion is that you avoid trying to remember more than is your learning style.

No matter on what a player is concentrating, he must keep one thing in mind — *the ball*. Whether at a Ping-Pong match or watching championship tennis at Wimbledon, you will hear players exhorting themselves to "watch the ball." Taking the eye off the ball probably accounts for more mistakes at every level than any other single cause. Good positioning, the right thought, and a correct swing are all useless unless the ball is met squarely.

Whenever you feel distracted, thinking about watching the ball will help bring you back to your basic level. Obviously, were you never to think of anything else you would not improve your game, but watching the ball stimulates concentration and frees your body to do what it has learned. It is a sort of general *montra* to the game and particularly useful during the warm-up when a player must get his eye on the ball even before he tries to psych out the major weaknesses in his opponent's game. Watching the ball is the main theme of good concentration.

The Ready Position. A beginner who can make use of a ball machine or has a friend who will toss evenly paced and placed balls to him is fortunate. He can begin to get the feel of his forward swing without having to get his racket and his body into position. Once a player knows how to swing forward, it is easier for him to create a backswing that will effectively set up his forward motion. If you are not so fortunate, you will have to be patient with the results of your shot while you learn to get your body in position and your racket back.

While waiting in the center of the backcourt for the ball, a standard *ready position* facing the net must be adopted so that you can react to a ball hit to either your forehand or your backhand. It is hardly likely that the ball will come right to you, so you must be in a crouching position to expedite a quick start toward it. Your weight should be on the balls of your feet, and your knees should be slightly bent. While such a position may be a little tiresome, in the end it will save you much wasted effort.

The racket should be held out in front of the body, pointing straight at the net, midway between a forehand and a backhand stroke (fig. 1 - 2). In order to prevent your arm from making any flourishes during the swing, you should hold your arm in a position

Figure 1-2

slightly bent at the elbow, a position that can be held almost throughout either a forehand or a backhand stroke. To keep the racket head from drooping or being held too upright ("cocked"), the left hand should cradle the throat of the racket near its head. Employing the left arm can help you to relax your racket arm and grip.

Grip Changing and Backswing Tips for Self-Starters. Since the backhand grip feels less natural to most neophytes, and is thus harder to find in a hurry, it is best to hold the racket in this grip in the ready position. Changing grips demands concentration until both grips feel familiar. The left hand can be used to turn the racket the necessary eighth of a turn. This should be done as soon as possible in conjunction with a turn of the wrist toward the forehand or the backhand side. (The wrist need not be bent again during the swing.)

Guiding the racket back, at least halfway, with both arms, keeps the shoulders turned sideways to the net and the racket head steady. The racket should be carried back almost as respect-fully as a cup of tea. When the racket is almost halfway back, you can begin to position yourself — deliberately, but no more slowly than if you were learning to tango. If the stroke is to be a forehand one, the racket arm can take the racket back until it is pointing straight toward the back fence.

Beginners who really have trouble getting to the ball after the first bounce should wait for the ball to get to them behind the base line. Only when the backswing and the forward swing begin to feel automatic should moving become a concern. Those who move well, but often miss the ball when they get to it, may be run-ning into the ball or hurrying their backswing. They should try to get "set" (stopped and with the racket back) before every shot, even it it means hitting some balls after the second bounce, at least until the strokes are grooved.

Hurrying one's strokes is almost certain to result in errors, so beginners should begin their backswings as soon as they can an-ticipate whether the ball is coming to their forehand or backhand. If you always feel rushed, thinking about taking your racket back should get top priority. When the ball is coming right at your body, choose immediately which stroke you will use.

Backswings also demand attention if some irregularity

affects the forward swing. Excessively bending or straightening the elbow or the wrist, opening or closing the racket face, taking the racket back too high or too low — are irregularities that usually proceed the forward motion and will affect the forward swing. It is easier to learn a whole new ready position and backswing than to work around a flaw.

Forming a habit of getting into the proper ready position and taking a deliberate backswing will have lasting benefits. A sloppy ready position and backswing are sure signs of poor concentration and balance, and they can ultimately interfere with stroke development and rhythm. Feigning an "unready look" will affect your game far more than your opponent's.

2

The Volley

If, as a complete beginner, you have taken my advice and begun hitting some volleys, you have probably dispelled some of the initial fears players often have about playing the net. Neglecting the net will only serve to inhibit you from taking that position, and thus curtail your learning to play an all-court game.

I hope that intermediates have experienced the fun of playing net. Even if you do not get much chance to volley (as few intermediates do in singles), practicing your volley will pay off. In the short run, volleying can help your ground strokes by sharpening your reactions and making you watch the ball. In the long run — you will have a better volley when you need it.

Admonitions to "watch the ball" and "block the ball" are not the only things you need to know about volleying at the net, but they are good for starters. However, before trying to absorb the more detailed instructions, you should first understand the simple theory behind net play.

THE DYNAMICS OF NET PLAY

In the backcourt a player may choose to do many things, but at net his aim should always be to win the point in one or two shots — the net is for the kill. It is hit or miss, pulling the trigger at the end of the hunt. Shooting quickly under pressure demands experience and practice. Of course, a good volleyer will demonstrate great skill, but a good volley need not be difficult.

In singles, a smart approach to the net and some speed are necessary, but in doubles, many a wise veteran can control the net if he anticipates well and has enough dexterity. Every step nearer the net offers the volleyer more angle and more opportunity to hit down into the court for a winner. This is the gravy of the game.

Unfortunately, winning is not all gravy. Statistics show that well over half of all points won are not made by winning shots, but are the results of opponents' errors. At the professional level of play, a smaller percentage of errors are made at the net than at the base line — the "batting average" is better there. This might not be true at other levels of play, but outside of the errors made in attempting to approach the net, or the volley errors forced after a weak approach, most volleys are missed because the player tries to make the shot *too good* or take *too much swing*. Too much swing is either a result of too much ambition or of too little know-how.

There are two reasons for not swinging at a volley. First, there is not enough time. After the ball leaves your opponent's racket, it travels only a little over half the distance it would travel to reach your base line. To swing at a volley requires a backswing, which takes more time than you usually have and commits you to hitting either a forehand or a backhand almost before you can anticipate on which side the ball is coming. Often the ball comes to neither side, but right at you.

The second reason for not swinging is simply that the swing is unnecessary, even for shots where time is available. Simply blocking the ball returns it with some of the speed that it carries. (Remember that a hard-hit ball is travelling faster before it bounces, unless the court is very fast.) Great speed on an angle volley would be likely to carry the ball too far. Whenever you are tempted to smash a high ball, remember that any high ball is also easy to angle. Swinging at a low volley is imprudent for the obvious reason that after the ball goes up over the net it must still come down in the court, a difficult proposition, angle or no. In the unforeseeable event that a volley had to be hit hard, a very hard shot can be hit by "jumping on the ball" (fig. 2 - 1). In this case, less swing than normal is needed.

Now that you know why you should not swing at a volley, you may be ready to learn more about *how* to keep from swinging. Regardless of your level of play, this section can improve your volley.

Figure 2-1

THE VOLLEY, EXECUTION

The waiting position at net is similar to the one you should use in the backcourt. The knees and back are bent slightly more to keep you in a lower position — in preparation for the greater number of low balls you will receive at net. The racket head should be halfway between the forehand and backhand stroke, shoulder high (well over the level of the net). The only other difference is that the racket is held as far out in front of you as it can be while still being supported by the left hand, just above the racket handle (fig. 2 - 2). The eastern forehand and backhand grips should be used.

Figure 2-2

NET RESULTS

When the ball comes, the wrist should bend to either side (forehand or backhand) or up (if the ball is high), until the racket face is almost open to the ball (parallel to the wrist). The arm remains in front of the body; and on the backhand, the opposite hand can be placed behind the racket throat to offer greater resistance to the impact. You do not meet the ball directly in front, which would be a little awkward (especially with the forehand). You hit it on a diagonal and step toward the net with your opposite leg as you make the shot (fig. 2 - 3).

Beginners should block the ball until they can not only connect solidly but also place the shot on either side of the court.

CHANGING GRIPS AT NET

Since Don Budge, there has been a controversy about whether or not players should use a single grip for both the forehand and backhand stroke. One argument for using the single grip — the "continental" — where the racket is grasped midway between the eastern forehand and backhand position, is based on a lack of time for changing grips. However, there are many players, good and bad, who find time to change grips, even at net, and changing grips has two advantages.

First, when the volley is executed with the continental grip, the angle of the racket face naturally opens, and the player is tempted to overslice in the effort to take the ball far out in front. Because you should always be trying to get closer to the net to increase your chances of hitting down into your opponent's court for the point, it is advantageous to meet the ball out in front as far as you can.

Second, and more important, the regular backhand grip increases the strength of the backhand stroke. Although you will not want to hit the ball as hard as you can, strength is needed for control and speed even when you are blocking the shot. The supreme importance of the backhand volley makes it advisable to use the strongest possible backhand grip.

The most difficult shots to handle at net are those that come right at the body. Ideally one is ready and will be able to move around a lot of these shots, but even the fastest players are caught at times. Less advanced players with sufficient time may also

Figure 2-3

bungle because they cannot decide whether to take the shot with a forehand or a backhand. There is a definite rule of thumb for this situation: Favor the backhand! For reasons obvious to a Ping-Pong player, (figs. 2 - 4 and 2 - 5) only the backhand stroke can be used to cover the body with a racket face open for blocking the ball. A two-handed backhand volley will not do (fig. 2 - 6). Remember, it is possible to hit almost any forehand with a backhand shot, but the reverse is not true.

For those who are used to the continental grip, the attempt to change may not be worth the effort. The grip controversy centers mostly around the beginner who has just learned the forehand and the backhand grips and is still struggling to change from one to the other. Why bring him to net and show him a third grip? Since he must learn to switch grips quickly enough to return serve, he might just as well practice the switch at net. But if he tries the continental grip at net, the beginner can get into bad habits at the base line. Most players who use the continental at net also use it for their ground strokes. This is not advised.

Figure 2-4   Figure 2-5   Figure 2-6

ADVANCING THE VOLLEY

After you have learned to switch grips with some success and to block an easy ball with some regularity, you may begin to "punch" the ball, employing a short follow-through. Unlike the follow-through of a ground stroke, your "punch" should be a slightly downward motion, unless of course the ball is below the level of the net when you hit it. Even after a hard put-away volley the racket should be no lower than waist high at the end of the swing (fig. 2 - 7). If you meet the ball far enough in front of your body, the open angle of the racket face should impart a gentle backspin to the shot. As you progress, you will want to make this backspin sharper and add some sidespin to your volleys. When you are hitting crosscourt, your racket can easily slice around the outside of the ball. Hitting a volley away from your body, down-the-line, is a less natural motion, but it will help if you think of slicing across the near side of the ball. These sidespins will slide an angle farther out of the court. Too much racket angle or chopping motion will make your shot bounce up too high, where it will "sit" a "set-up" for your opponent. A good volley will slide low and force your opponent to get way down to the ball and hit up to your "put-away" volley.

Figure 2-7

3

The Backhand

BACKHAND STRENGTH

If you are a beginner and have started by volleying at the net, the backhand stroke is the ground stroke you should be working on first. The backhand is almost as important when you are playing in the backcourt as when you're at net. Since it is more difficult to learn than the forehand, a headstart is valuable — backhands, even more than volleys, suffer from neglect. If the volley seemed easy, perhaps you are ready for the challenge.

Among intermediates there is a prevalent notion that the backhand should be a more "natural" stroke than the forehand. Yet, the backhand is the nemesis of nine out of ten intermediate players. Some very advanced players find the backhand easier to perfect, but it is rarely easier to learn. Often beginners are started with the forehand stroke because it is feared that trouble with the backhand might discourage them from learning the game. The reason the backhand is so difficult is that it requires a unique strength.

Even the muscular beginner who has quickly mastered the backhand grip and swing will have to struggle to maintain half the speed of his forehand drives. Certain muscles in the elbow and wrist must be developed before the backhand stroke can be executed with any power. Since these muscles are used only for backhands they are often strained and result in a condition almost unique to tennis players, namely, "tennis elbow."

THE GRIP

When they first hold a racket, most people use an eastern forehand grip, a "shaking hands" grasp, with the palm of the hand and the forearm behind the racket providing strength. But try to hit a backhand with this grip; you will notice that the racket must be pulled through the swing with the tips of the fingers and the top of the thumb. The arm is in front of the racket (fig. 3 - 1). A mountain climber might find this backhanded awkwardness challenging, but Francoise Durr is the only professional player who uses this grip with regularity. Considerations of grace aside, its use makes it very difficult for her to hit high balls.

By turning your hand an eighth around the racket from the forehand grip, you will find the correct backhand grip position (fig. 3 - 2). The side of the thumb, almost from the wrist down, is behind the racket on the small bevel; the forearm position is automatically altered so that it is no longer necessary to drag the racket through the swing behind the arm. This new position is not a "natural" one — a beginner would not discover it quickly on his own — but its awkwardness is due to a lack of strength and to the closed position of the racket "face." Only a difficult turn of the wrist will aim the ball over the net unless the ball is met a foot or so in front of the body. This brings us to the swing.

THE SWING FOR THE BACKHAND DRIVE

Tell a beginner to swing naturally and he will swing the racket in a half-circle around his body. Such a swing is easy to control, just as it is easy to draw a steady curve in the sand by keeping the arm extended in a round compasslike swing around the body. However, if a player is to meet the ball in front of his body and direct it straight over the net, his swing must be straightened (diagram 1) or he must turn more than ninety degrees sideways from the net. As such a turn is not always timely, a recipe for the desired straightened forward motion is given below.

After getting the proper backhand grip, stand sideways and let the racket arm hang down across the body against the back thigh with the racket pointing to the back fence. The racket will be parallel to the ground just below waist level. The throat of the

Figure 3-1

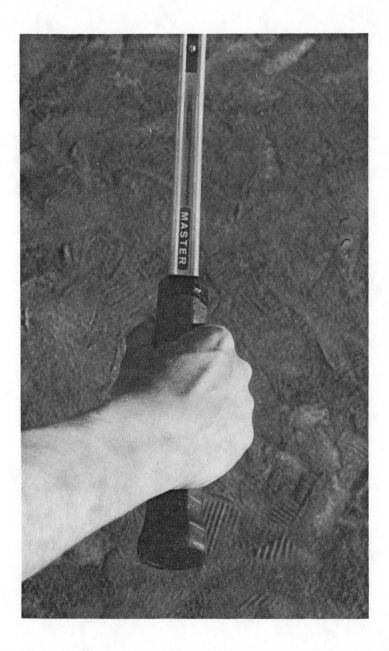

Figure 3-2

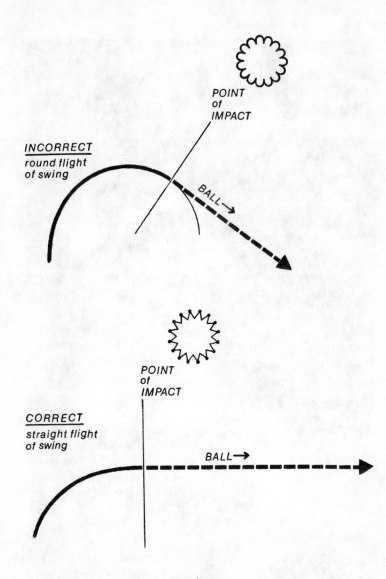

Diagram 1
THE SWING

racket (near the head) should be held firmly in the fingers of the left hand, which will be a great help in bringing the racket back and down, and perhaps in giving it a little push forward. With knees slightly bent, weight on the balls of the feet (the feet close together), and the back straight, wait for the ball. (See Fig. 3 - 3). Begin the forward swing as if to batter the ball with the butt end of the racket handle. This will prevent the arm from swinging out from (and thus around) the body. In order to meet the ball, the wrist must come around gradually, as though you were throwing a frisbee to a child. The racket face is a foot in front of the body at impact. (Fig. 3 - 4 — notice the front foot has stepped forward into the ball.) So straight is the swing that the ball, should it be missed, would come within a racket length of the body (fig. 3 - 5).

You should push the racket "through" the ball, and the arm and the racket should point directly ahead at the end of the follow-through. The racket head will be about head-high (fig. 3 - 6). If the ball is slow and between waist-high and knee-high, the stroke should produce results. But remember to meet the ball low, using a pendulum-like motion. I have never seen a pupil who could not hit several perfect backhands in this way during the first lesson. Even a slender child of eight can manage it, if positioned no more than fifteen feet from the net.

If a beginner were able to anticipate in what direction the ball was coming, get in perfect position, and be sure that the ball would come slowly enough to time the swing, strength would not be such a necessity. Although a pro who has never developed any special strength in his left arm can hit an intermediate left-handed backhand off a relatively slow ball just because of his expert anticipation, the beginner, to whom all balls seem fast, will swing too late, too far away, or when he is off-balance, leaving him to wonder if he will ever master this easy swing. If you are not perfectly positioned, it takes timing and a strong arm to control the ball.

The frustration of trying to hit (not block) a backhand drive often tempts players to compromise their stroke by using faulty techniques that increase strength, or give that illusion.

Figure 3-3

Figure 3-4

Figure 3-5

Figure 3-6

FAULTY TECHNIQUES

The "Round-House Swing. It is amazing how many players let the racket make a half circle around their body, thinking that because the racket gets swishing fast with momentum, they can utilize its power. Unfortunately like the home-run swing in baseball, the shot is hit or miss. Everyone knows the percentage of the all-or-nothing baseball slugger. In tennis there is no sure home run, and thus no percentage.

The ball cannot be met a foot in front of the body and directed to the middle of the opponent's court with a round swing, unless the body is turned more than ninety degrees sideways to the net. Such a turn is desirable only when the ball is so far to the side that the player can barely reach it by stepping parallel to the net. (Fig. 3 - 7.)

Unless your muscles are abnormally well-developed for backhands (after years of furious frisbee throwing), there are two real drawbacks to a round swing. First, turning more than ninety degrees is apt to encourage you to step parallel to the net — too much across the flight of the ball. This can make balance difficult for players who lack strong arms and an excellent sense of timing to add power to their backhand by the push of their weight. In an effort to augment power, the player will "break" his wrist and lose control.

Or, second, the player using a round swing will connect with the ball with his arm extended far out to the side of his body and, without an arm of iron, the player's wrist will fold a little at impact, imparting a slight slice. The shoulders must help bring the racket through the ball by opening (turning) toward the net. This shoulder motion also brings the racket face across the ball, increasing the slice.

Although the stock-in-trade of the backhand stroke is a good slice, such as that used by advanced players returning a serve or making an approach shot, the slice will not evolve quickly from the round swing. It is a rather sophisticated shot, demanding a timing and a feel for the racket which can only be acquired from a basic drive. In addition to demanding a backhand strength, the slice is not powerful enough to suffice in all situations; passing shots, for example. The beginner is best off trying to strengthen his arm for a straight backhand drive.

Figure 3-7

The Two-Handed Backhand. Partly because of the recent fame of child prodigy Chris Evert, the two-handed backhand is enjoying a vogue among junior players who want to imitate the power drive from the base line. The strength gained from using two hands is considerable for a beginner and changing to a backhand grip becomes unnecessary. However, without remarkable coordination the shot is awkward and inefficient. With both hands on the racket, lateral reach, near as well as far, is reduced (fig. 3 - 8) and low balls demand a stooping, twisted posture.

In order to put backspin on the ball with a two-handed backhand, the "back" hand must be dropped or used almost exclusively, which many two-handers are reluctant to attempt. A few pros, mostly men — notably Jimmy Connors, Frew McMillan and Pancho Segura — are able to use backspin effectively with two-handed strokes, but this is not to assume that any mortal could master the task. Of these pros, only McMillan prefers the net — where backspin is a must. Most two-handers settle for a bad backhand volley, which works to keep them away from the net even when they should be there (on fast courts and in doubles). They become dependent on their two-handed drive, which is often violently topspun to keep the ball in the court. Since exertion is difficult to time, the result is a larger percentage of mis-hit shots.

Most aspiring juniors would do better to imitate Chris Evert's exemplary concentration and work habits rather than to try to mimick her unique style. There will be good players emerging with her strokes, but it is unlikely that any will be as successful as she against the rising number of players with the all-court effectiveness of Billie Jean King and Margaret Court. Only very small players may need two hands, and the eventual size of a junior player is hard to predict — look now at "tiny" Chris Evert.

The Poke Backhand (The Hinge Elbow). One of the most common backhand faults, especially among beginning and intermediate women, is the "poke." The player leads the swing with the elbow, usually held high, and then pokes the ball by straightening the elbow. Poking provides a modicum of power but demands awkward bending to retrieve low balls (fig. 3 - 9) and is tricky to time on fast balls. Unlike the two-handed backhand, the poke is not a serious shot. Its follow-through is hopelessly aborted.

Figure 3-8

Figure 3-9

Convincing those who poke that they *should* change is not a problem. Players usually know if they poke the ball, and if they don't know, the grip is often a tell-tale sign. Watch for the thumb flat up the back of the racket (fig. 3 - 10).

Changing a poke is another matter. It means giving up whatever proficiency was achieved — at best a good low chop — and starting all over again. Neither the poke nor the two-handed backhand builds the necessary muscles in the arm to allow for easy change in hitting a proper backhand.

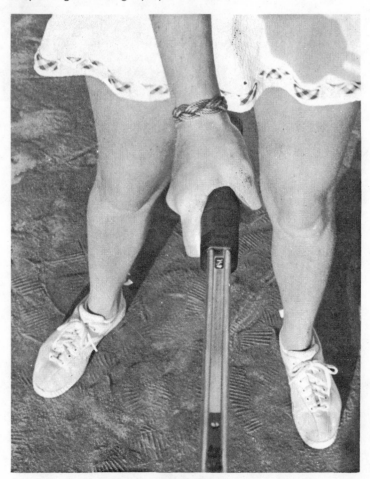

Figure 3 - 10

BACKHAND STRENGTHENING EXERCISES

Pancho Gonzales wrote in his biography that the two-handed backhand might add strength, but that it was twice as hard to learn. Any player, with the timing and dexterity to master the two-handed backhand, can certainly master a one-handed swing, given a little patience to acquire strength.

Strengthening the arm for the backhand is not an onerous task. The best way, of course, is to hit many backhands. Part of the reason backhands do not develop is because they are avoided. Players "run around" their backhands and invariably start rallies with their forehands. If starting a rally with your backhand is difficult, then your backhand needs work.

The best place to practice starting a rally with your backhand is at the backboard. At first, stand not too far from the wall (maybe twenty feet) and try to hit the ball softly, so it will be easy to hit again. If you think you can hit it hard, but have trouble adjusting to a slower pace, you have probably been swinging too wildly (a "round-house"?). Control demands more strength than power.

Start by standing sideways to the board with your feet close together, holding the ball a foot off your front shoulder and your racket back, below waist level, pointing straight away from the board. The arms are crossed with the racket arm below (fig. 3 - 11). If you relax, the position will not feel so awkward. Toss the ball up about a foot out of your hand, trying to have it bounce about a foot and a half in front of you toward the board and a racket-length out to the side. Step forward with your front foot and start swinging when the ball hits the court (fig. 3 - 12). Your racket should meet the ball after it has dropped to between waist and knee level from the top of its bounce. Hit softly up on the ball so that it will return straight to your backhand. Once you can do this with some consistency, which shouldn't take more than a day or two on the average, you should try to keep a rally going at the same soft speed. As you get better you will have to do less running. Practice fifteen to thirty minutes a day, and in a week you should be able to maintain a rally of from five to ten shots. Then move back a few feet and work toward the same goal. Counting will be an important help to your concentration, but don't do it every time. Think about taking the racket back immediately after every shot and swinging through correctly.

Figure 3-11   Figure 3-12

Done almost daily over a period of a month or two, this backboard exercise will do more than anything else to strengthen your arm for the backhand. Although it may seem a rather placid drill at first, getting into good position will keep your feet very busy, and hitting backhand after backhand is strenuous exercise for the arm. Do not practice this drill for more than fifteen minutes a day without frequent rests. If at any point your arm feels very fatigued or numb, rest immediately — tendons can be painfully pulled from persistent overhitting. (See Chapter 14). This exercise is also an excellent aid in grooving your swing.

4

The Well-Tempered Forehand

While you've been struggling to put zip into your backhand, or even if you're only beginning tennis, you will probably be hoping to have more of those zippy forehand drives stay in the court. If you are an intermediate, your forehand may thrive against the well-tempered ball of a better player, or look great in warm-ups. On your best day you might have put holes in your opponent and walked off the court feeling like a weekend Arthur Ashe. But in your deepest moments — say, when you are losing to a player you thought was half your speed in the warm-up — you may feel that your subconscious is playing against you, reminding you of your percentages. The result will be the "choke," that phenomenon familiar to everyone who has ever been in a pressure situation in sports. To choke sometimes in a crucial situation is human. However, if you keep getting into choke situations when you don't think you should be, it is not because you are an habitual choke, but because something fundamental is wrong with your game.

The most common problem with forehands is that they are overhit. It is easy to assume that because you can feel a hard forehand in a rally, it will be your strength in a match and win for you. Unfortunately, matches are not won so much as lost — even at world championship levels, it is a rare match when over fifty percent of all points are not "won" on errors. A shot must become nearly error-proof before it can become a strength.

Decreasing the number of errors is not just a matter of hitting the ball softer. You will win if you make fewer errors than your opponent, but your opponent may not make errors if you do not force them. Furthermore, there are a large number of players who claim they cannot ease up on the throttle without falling to pieces. These born sluggers go through life cursing the cut-artist and the soft-baller (there is also a smaller breed of gentle people who cannot bear to hit the ball hard) and usually complain that if they only had a little more time to practice "they'd blast all the pushers off the court." Well, we've all heard some idle boasting. The weekend Arthur Ashe is going to be a perennial choke, losing to all except other weekend sluggers and a few push-overs and novices who might be intimidated in the warm-ups.

The fate of the slugger is unnecessary because there is a trick — topspin — which makes forcing drives drop more consistently into the court. Topspin is taught and used by millions of players — even the real sharpshooters like Arthur Ashe and Chris Evert (especially on her two-handed backhand). You could practice hitting flat drives for years and still lack the control topspin will give you in one-tenth of the time. There are also a number of great underspin drives (Rosewall's backhand being the best), but underspin is a more sophisticated weapon demanding excellent timing as well as more experience. Topspin is the staple of all forehand drives, and as such it is as crucial to the beginning forehand as gaining strength in the arm is to the beginning backhand.

THE BEAUTY OF TOPSPIN

An overspinning (topspun) ball drops faster than a flat or underspun ball. This means that a drive can be hit with a greater margin of safety over the net and that it can still drop with more margin before the base line. The price you seem to pay for this double error-saver is a slower drive. However, comparing the dynamics of the drives' flights, the topspinning ball has more pace after the bounce. The ball will "jump" and hit your opponent's racket "heavier" than a flat drive.

It is not often that we can "have our cake and eat it, too."

THE SIMPLICITY OF TOPSPIN

Beginners usually think that all spin is very tricky and, admittedly, a heavy spin can be tricky, because the flight of the racket comes across the flight of the ball for only a very short time

— making mis-hitting (or even missing completely) a strong likelihood. But a gentle (and helpful) topspin is as basic to tennis as a slight spiral is to football throwing, or as "English" is to billiards. A tennis ball rarely comes off the racket without some spin, and the effect can be dramatically visible. Since the ball is soft, the flight of the ball is changed not only by the spin but also by the resulting momentary distortion in the shape of the ball as it leaves the racket.

Dramatic effects are achieved by advanced racket actions, but the helpful topspin can be applied to a drive by a complete beginner. Most coaches have an easy top spin rule for players of all abilities: start the forward swing with the racket a foot lower than the level where you intend to hit the ball, and end the swing a foot higher. A more exact description of how to execute this drive will follow this section.The "tricky" part is to get your racket and body in position with plenty of time left to execute your swing.

THE FOREHAND DRIVE (GRIP AND SWING)

First grip the racket with an eastern forehand grip (figs 4-1A and 4-1B). If you have not read the first chapter of this book, you should do so to catch up on the method of taking the racket back from the ready position. Because those preparations were discussed at length there, we need only stress here that the backswing brings the racket *down* below the intended level of impact with the ball. This must be stressed for two reasons.

First, if you start the forward swing with the racket at the same level or about that of the ball, "brushing up" (as Ed Faulkner says) or "wiping up" (as Jack Barnaby says) on the ball becomes less natural and complete, if not impossible. A slice is more apt to result.

Second, because the player is watching the ball and cannot see peripherally where the racket is at the back of the swing, it can be very difficult to feel whether or not the racket is down.

For this reason Ed Faulkner, after forty years of teaching experience, has found it easier to teach topspin to players of all calibers by starting them with their rackets already back and down. He excepted pupils from this practice only after they had developed or demonstrated a backswing that was already grooved

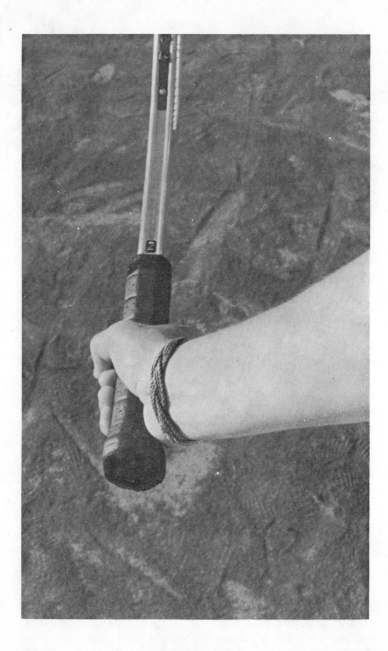

Figure 4-1A

Figure 4-1B

to get the racket back to the same low spot. Once a pupil had gotten the feel of brushing up on the ball, the back-down position could serve as a point of reference — if after incorporating a backswing he could no longer feel his strings brushing up on the ball, then the racket had not been started sufficiently far down. This method was more successful than trying to convince a player to make his backswing take the racket down in order to get the feel of meeting the ball in a way that he had never experienced with the old swing. The Faulkner method not only makes it easier to get this new feel, but it also makes it easier to get the feel of taking the racket down in back.

When the racket is down behind you, it should be pointing at the back fence, the racket face straight up and down, and the racket head parallel with the grip (no droop — see fig 4-2). As a comfortable height to meet the ball will be waist-high or below, "down" means a foot below that. This means bending your knees.

The most important thing to notice in the photograph is that the racket arm is not fully straightened, the way you would like it to be for the backhand. Instead, the elbow and wrist should be bent slightly as shown, until contact with the ball is made. This "sideways, down and back" position should be meticulously imitated by beginners anxious to improve their consistency and accuracy in starting rallies with the forehand.

Part of improving your start is in the toss; reaching after a badly tossed ball can ruin your swing. With the elbow of your tossing arm slightly bent, cup the ball in your palm as though it were a piece of cake. Don't jerk the ball up into the air or just drop it — lift it up gently — and don't try to hit it before it bounces. If you toss it into the air a foot or so out of your hand, it should bounce to about waist high (allowing you to take your time). You will have plenty of time if you hit the ball as it is dropping from the height of its bounce, when it feels most comfortable. If you aim the toss to bounce toward the net post (away from you), a single step toward the net should bring you to within a comfortable distance. Proceed with the swinging and hitting motions described below.

This starting position is natural, but if any bad habit was previously developed, the wrist and elbow should be "locked" into these angles in the "ready position," from which the arm can be brought back mostly by turning the body. Now we can see the importance, mentioned in the section on the "ready position" in

Figure 4-2

39

Chapter 1, of waiting in a specific and constant ready position. By taking the racket back with the turn of the body sideways, the elbow and wrist position can be maintained and the player does not have to think of two separate actions in turning and getting the racket back.

Once in the "down" position, you should try to hold yourself sideways as long as you can, while the shoulder and upper arm bring the racket across the body. It is this effort that makes the forehand look less natural than the backhand, where only the wrist is turned to come around to the ball, and the arm swings freely through without causing the shoulder to turn toward the net. In the forehand, however, as in the serve or any throwing motion, the opening (turning) of the shoulders toward the net adds considerable power to the motion. This power, in turn, makes positioning the feet slightly less important with the forehand than with the backhand. Balance and power can be maintained with an open or closed stance, although beginners and intermediates should avoid either extreme. The open stance will cause a beginner's racket to come off the ball too soon, and the closed stance will jeopardize either balance or power.

In the shock-absorbing follow-through, the elbow must be straightened while the wrist remains back as a "cushion" behind the ball. The ball should be met parallel to the front leg (fig. 4-3) and *pushed*.

Concentrating on pushing the ball will help you get the feel of "wiping up" the back of the ball with the strings. In the beginning, merely think of following through to a point as far out and as straight toward the net as you can (fig 4-4). To make certain that you are extending your follow-through, give it a definite end — "freeze" as if the action had been stopped on film, then examine it to see how far it has gone. Your arm should be straight and your wrist should not have turned more than ninety degrees since the "cushion" position (less than it turns in the backhand). The racket should be pointing to the area of the court to which you have hit the ball, and the racket head should be about head-high, higher than the grip. Exaggerating this finish (as a golfer holds his follow-through after a shot) will improve your concentration and increase your follow-through. Thus you will gain control faster. The steps described will soon become automatic.

Figure 4-3

Figure 4-4

COMMON FAULTY TECHNIQUES

Straight-arming — The Price You Pay. Many people who haven't learned to "push" the ball with the elbow bent and the wrist cushioned adopt a straight-arm, "no fault" forehand swing. I say "no fault" because once this forehand swing is started, there is no adjusting it. Like "no fault" auto insurance, the point is to reduce hassles rather than provide special compensation when it is needed. Since they can't "feel" the ball with the arm in this position, their good shots, given a fair sense of timing, seem to hit themselves.

Unfortunately, errors are unavoidable for straight-armers if any last second adjustment is needed. Players complain endlessly about bad bounces and tricky winds, but the plain facts are that even indoors every swing needs frequent adjustment — inevitably we end up with less time than we'd like to swing at the ball. Straight-arming takes up entirely too much time and it leaves the body vulnerable (as a boxer's body is left open by a "round-house" swing). Returning serve hurries every player, and a straight-arm hitter should be beaten by any opponent who can hit a hard serve right at him. The ability to adjust at the last second also provides a necessary disguise for some very advanced "touch" shots ("drops"), which would be difficult to control without the caressing ("cushioning") follow-through of a bent arm.

The Poke, Chop, Slice, and "Flat" Drive. Poking is straight-arming's opposite, a habit developed by that gentle breed who cannot stand to swing at the ball too hard. The elbow is very bent, the arm from the elbow down is used in a poking motion. Easiest of all methods to adopt, it offers no chance for much advancement. The remedy for the backhand poke, you will remember, was to straighten the arm. Although this remedy means adopting (for a time) the undesirable straight-arm forehand, there is no other way to reverse the poke.

The chop is a sliced poke, a violent underspin or sidespin slice. Although the chop takes too much pace off the ball to be an advanced shot (and leaves the ball sitting in the air for your opponent to smash), it is an "advanced" fault in that it usually develops from a poke or a slice. The violent action of chopping demands some timing and feel, and the chopper may think he is quite the tricky cut-artist. This will make him even more reluctant to undertake the cure — learning a new swing (with a straight-arm if necessary).

Virtually every ball that is not top spun will be underspun, or sliced. The slice may be very slight, but as I have said, it is almost impossible to hit a ball without putting spin on it. Most players who think they are hitting *flat* are not. Chances are they are confusing the lack of margin over the net with hitting flat, in which event, they are definitely slicing. A sliced ball stays more consistently low to the net than any other shot.

The problem with a slice, however, is not in keeping the ball low to the net, but in keeping it from rising and sailing out of the court. A slight topspin permits more margin for error over the net and brings the ball down into the court. Since the swing for the slight top spin and the swing for the slight slice do not appear to differ greatly, it can be hard for the inexperienced player to see or feel the difference. Thus it is often necessary to exaggerate the change from the problem slice in order to cure what seems to be a "slight" problem. Continuing to play with this "slight" slice is as silly as encouraging a common cold to linger. Recommended — a heavy dose of top spin.

The Continental Forehand. You might guess that because the continental grip (fig. 4 - 5) can be used for serves, backhands, forehands and net it was developed and perfected by someone anxious to avoid learning to change grips. Actually the grip developed because there was a need — now almost obsolete — to handle ground strokes on a grass court, where the ball bounces very low. Some experts date this grip back to the thirties and to Don Budge, who used it almost to perfection in his famous backhand. If one wants to consider court tennis, the game of kings, the continental grip probably dates back hundreds of years. In court tennis, where the ball is not at all bouncy, the object is to slice every ball hard enough to make it skid. In tennis, even on grass, a slice is not sufficient for every shot (passing shots especially) because the ball is much livelier. On any surface except grass, using the continental grip will force you to slice the higher bouncing balls, sometimes to disadvantage, since the angle of the racket face opens (tilts back) more and more as you lift your arm. Although you may not have strength to do other than slice a high backhand, you should want to drive a high forehand.

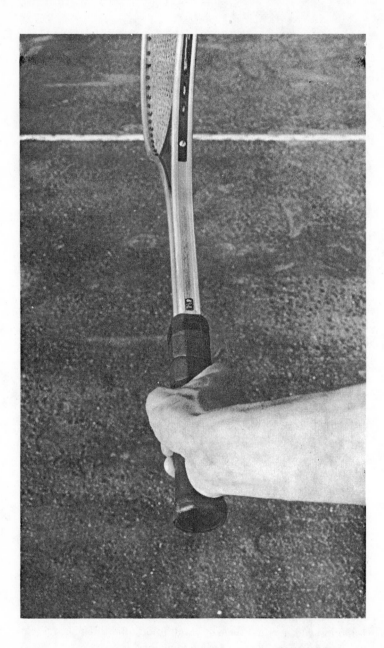

Figure 4-5

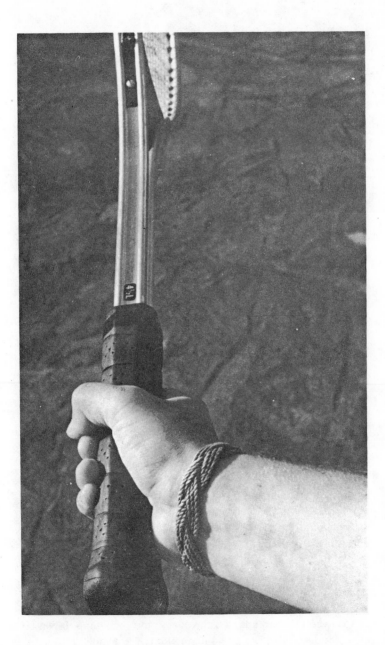

Figure 4-6

NET RESULTS

The Western Forehand. More common today than the continental variation of the forehand grip is the western grip (fig. 4 - 6), which tilts the racket angle over the opposite way (closed). As you might guess, the western grip makes it easier to drive high balls and was developed to advantage on high bouncing surfaces by short players. "Little Bill" Johnston, the most noted advocate of the western grip, came from the high bouncing, hard courts of California in the twenties. Not surprisingly, many of the short "westerners" are women, notably Chris Evert. But because of the disadvantages involved in using the western forehand, taller players are silly to use it; and the smaller men, like Eddie Dibbs, have not been able to use it successfully against the net rushers of today. The success of Little Bill's western forehand against backcourt players belongs to another era.

Except for its effectiveness in driving high balls, the only advantage in using the western forehand is to impart a more violent topspin with a straighter swing and less effort. Since less effort often demands less strength, women and children again have more excuse for using the western forehand. This is true only of balls of medium height, where the western grip has tilted the racket face over at just the right angle to make top spin inevitable on a straight swing. The advantage comes in a hurried situation where topspin might allow a looser swing and make it possible to hit a more offensive shot from what is basically a defensive position. It takes an advanced player to understand when such a situation might occur. The most likely time for such a tactic is when your opponent is approaching net or forcing you with a strong shot, like a serve. Returning power with power is not, however, your only answer, even on a fast, high bouncing surface. On most surfaces, especially grass, it is generally considered a poor percentage shot. The timing of such returns on grass was thought impossible until the Czech, Jan Kodes, beat Stan Smith to reach the finals of Forest Hills against John Newcombe in 1973. Although Kodes had just won a weakened Wimbledon and had been a finalist before, he was not highly seeded on grass. With big, driving returns, he had won recognition as one of the finest clay-court players in the world, but while even the mighty swingers like Ashe and Newcombe had adopted the slice return part-time to win on grass, Kodes worked to prove them wrong. He almost did — taking Newcombe to five sets before losing. Kodes, incidentally, does not use a western grip. The most phenomenal western forehand belongs to Bjorn Borg, and it remains to be seen how it will hold up on grass.

Regardless of the value of the western tactic for returning serves, a practice which again has a larger following among women, the western grip creates problems for the beginner and places severe limitations on the best of players. The angle of the racket face at knee level is closed to such a degree as to demand either a violent swing and a difficult turn of the wrist, or a bend of the knees so deep that only Francoise Durr would attempt it (and not even she could recover quickly enough after it). The angle of the racket face almost precludes a slice at any height, forcing the player to drive from the middle of the court and to change grips for the volley, which, you will remember, must be sliced. In addition, because of the number of balls which come to your feet at net, using a western grip there becomes impossible. Not surprisingly, most westerners, even the aggressive ones, try to win the point before a volley is necessary. And ordinarily, westerners never learn to volley well. Thus Chris Evert, who arrived in the semis at Forest Hills without any volley at all, has practiced her net game — her concession to the more orthodox methods of other top women professionals (and to her recent physical growth).

Women and children, especially girls, often happen upon the western grip because it lets the racket head droop, and therefore requires less strength. A very tough habit to break, it has an early and lasting influence on a player's game. In addition to limiting a player's forehand both in the backcourt and at net, the western grip can have an effect on the backhand as well, since the western grip is located so far from the backhand grip that a major motion must be made when it is necessary to change. Some beginners prefer to turn the racket over and execute the phenomenon dubbed "same-sidedness" by Ed Faulkner. Despite the limitations of this bizarre backhand, the shot survives at an intermediate club level. Many westerners prefer a two-handed backhand, where the forehand grip does not have to be changed. The power added in a two-handed backhand helps to make the stroke a favorite of smaller players. Dynamically, the problems of the two-handed backhand are similar to those of the western forehand.

5

The Serve

Unique only to the serve is the synchronization of two movements — tossing the ball with one arm and hitting it with the other. No matter how coordinated you are, the exact timing and execution needed for a good serve will present problems and demand a practiced rhythm.

Players who have little or no experience serving should approach their first attempt with a general idea of the motion and its purpose, and as little specific advice as possible. Trying to execute your first attempts "by the book" could inhibit any natural actions you might perform. It would be better to get a picture of the serve before you try it by watching a more experienced player of your own age, sex, build, and general athletic ability. Imitating a real serve will be easier than trying to create a good motion from looking at still photographs in a book.

Were you to begin learning the serve with help from a professional, chances are he would ask you to throw a ball over the net from the base line before letting you attempt your first serves. Just throwing the ball will illustrate the basic idea of serving to the pupil, and it gives the instructor an indication of how well the pupil should perform. Beginners start at all stages in serving, and in different ways, but there is a definite correlation between one's throwing skills and the quickness with which the serve can be learned. If you throw well, you will probably learn to serve quickly with a minimum of advice. A professional may merely ask you to hold the racket with an eastern forehand grip (fig. 5 - 1) and to stand sideways to the net with your serving arm nearest the back fence when you begin your motion. You may also want to take a few practice swings, pretending that you are throwing the racket into the service blocks. Or, if the pro thinks he knows your

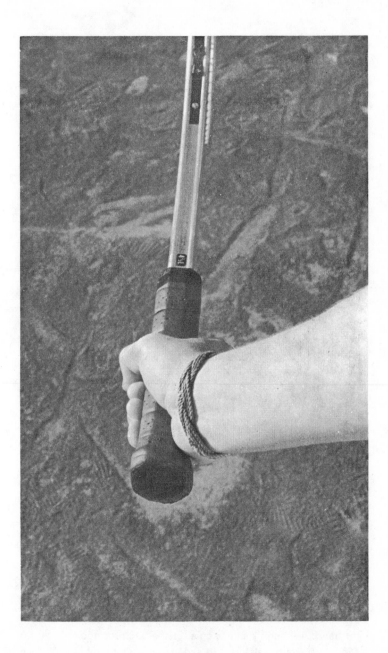

Figure 5-1

capabilities, he may demonstrate a serve he feels you can imitate. Any other explanation can await the results of your first attempts.

Although being able to throw a ball well is a definite advantage in learning to serve, it is not a prerequisite. Millions of players have learned good serves without being ex-Little Leaguers (Europeans, who grew up kicking soccer balls, and women). When they are learning to serve, however, those who have little throwing experience may have some problems tossing the ball and will need to study the following descriptions closely, after they have tried their hand at imitation. Throwers, also, will want to study the service motion in detail, especially those parts of the motion which are of some immediate concern.

While the toss and the backswing should be performed simultaneously in the first half of the service motion, the two steps can be practiced separately from each other and separately from the second half of the serve, when the ball is actually hit. The best way to describe a serve, and sometimes the best way to begin learning a serve (especially for a player who is having difficulty connecting solidly with the ball), is to begin with the toss. An erratic toss is the most common cause for beginning service problems and bad service habits.

THE TOSS AND STANCE — STEP 1

It is essential to be able to toss the ball the same way and to the same point every time, otherwise the great advantage of the serve — complete control of the ball — is lost. A serve is similar to a personal signature — it should be executed in the same way every time, and learning to serve without an accurate toss is almost as difficult as learning to write your name with the paper moving about. While tossing is not simple, it is an easily perfected motion if done correctly.

In tossing, you should keep your hand under the ball and rest the ball between your thumb and index and middle fingers; the second ball will rest in the palm of your hand (fig. 5 - 2). Holding the ball this way will enable you to toss the ball exactly where you want it, which will be, at most, eighteen inches straight up from your hand. Although most people let the ball drop too low before hitting it, they also release it too soon and toss it too high. The ball

Figure 5-2

should be hit at the top of your reach, which should be at the top of the toss when the ball is neither rising nor falling. By tossing too high and waiting for the ball to drop, you increase your chances of mis-hitting because the ball is falling across the flight of your racket. Waiting for the ball can also cause a hitch in your motion, killing the momentum — the raison d'etre — of your backswing. By reaching as high as you can for the ball, you get your maximum angle to hit over the net down into the service blocks.

Believe it or not, it may help to practice this finger-tip toss: play a sort of basketball against anything a couple of feet over your reach. On the court, you should adopt a server's stance to practice the toss. To serve to the left service block, you would stand just to the right of the center of the court, and behind the base line. With your left foot several inches behind the line, point it toward the net post on the right half of the court. Put your right foot about six inches behind your left foot parallel to the base line. You will be sideways to the net. To serve to the other service block, start on the other half of your court. A line drawn tangential to the toes of your sneakers should point into whichever service block you are aiming (diagram 2).

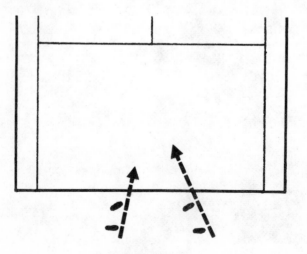

Diagram 2
SERVICE STANCE

Figure 5-3

Before tossing, aim your racket toward the service block you would be serving into, and place your tossing hand under the racket's throat to support the racket head. Your racket arm should be almost straight, while your tossing arm is slightly bent at the elbow, (Fig. 5 - 3). Notice the elbow of the tossing arm points toward the ground to keep the hand under the ball. Bring both arms down where they would fall naturally, so that your tossing arm almost bounces off your front thigh. Then push the tossing arm right back up with your shoulder, releasing the ball when your hand is over head-high. Let the ball drop in order to see if the toss is going as nearly straight up and down as possible. The ball should land about twelve inches ahead of you, in the same direction the toes of your front foot are pointing. A toss which goes straight up and down has less chance of getting away from you than a toss which arcs across your head, either parallel or perpendicular to the base line.

When you achieve some accuracy with this practice toss, try to synchronize it with more of a swing. After the racket arm goes down with the tossing arm, swing it back (toward the fence behind

Figure 5-4

the court), then up loosely, until your arm is almost parallel to the court and the racket is pointing up (fig. 5 - 4). If you don't like this golflike backswing, and many players do not, bring your arm up so that it is pointing more toward the fence on the right side of the court. In either case the wrist can be swung back (Stan Smith's and Billie Jean King's method) or held cocked (Chris Evert's and John Newcombe's method). Once you have the rhythm of what Ed Faulkner called the "down-together - up-together" backswing, the rest of the service motion may follow more naturally.

HITTING THE BALL — Step 2

If your service toss is in control, but you have trouble timing your swing or connecting with the ball solidly, you should adopt an abbreviated swing as a step in learning to serve. One popular swing begins from the "backscratcher" position (fig. 5 - 5). The wrist is bent back to position the racket head by the lower back, as shown in the photograph, and the butt of the racket handle points up toward where the ball will be tossed. The elbow is bent and points towards the side fence, and the upper arm runs parallel to the base line. The grip and stance are the same as described earlier. With your weight on your back foot, toss the ball up, well in front of you. Bring the racket head up with your arm and your wrist, and shift your weight to the toes of your front foot by turning your shoulders toward the net. Reach up high, as if to swat an insect — as high above your head as you can reach (fig. 5 - 6). At contact with the ball, let your wrist snap over (fig. 5 - 7) and follow through down to the left side of your front ankle (fig. 5 - 8).

You should notice that you are not hitting the ball flat. A completely flat serve is not desirable for reasons that will be made obvious later. If you feel that you are hitting the ball flat, check your grip before and after each swing to make certain that it is not slipping to a western forehand grip (a flat serve is not possible with an eastern forehand grip). If you feel you are spinning the ball too much, you are probably pulling your racket too much across the back or side of the ball from left to right. Take a practice toss to see if you are not tossing too far to the right, and then try to hit more straight into the ball without worrying at first about where it goes. You can learn to compensate with your wrist for any small tendency your serves may have to go down and to the left.

Figure 5-5

Figure 5-6

Figure 5-7

Figure 5-8

NET RESULTS

To hit a satisfactory serve from the backscratcher start requires strength (there is no momentum from a backswing), but the result is not necessarily the reason for the step. Even if your serve never quite gets over the net, the backscratcher illustrates in a simple way what happens in the second half of the swing. After working on the toss and the backscratcher, every player will be ready to attempt a motion with a backswing and a follow-through.

THE COMPLETE SERVE — Step 3

Splicing the "down-together - up-together" toss and backswing motions with the backscratcher is mostly a matter of timing and rhythm. If you think you might be ready to try step 3, do not be discouraged if you do not connect solidly with the ball. To connect at all during your first serves is promising. If you have no luck, you may want to go over what should be done and take some practice swings without a ball (some quickly and some slowly) in front of a mirror.

With your upper arm parallel to the ground, try to bend your elbow to get the racket into the backscratcher position while starting to turn your shoulders toward the net. The racket may not "fall" naturally into the backscratcher position, but at least a lesser dip should occur (perhaps more the result of your wrist bending). If you get the racket deep into the backscratcher, a hitch (a stop in your motion) will probably occur until you have the knack of timing the turn of your shoulders.

FAULTY TECHNIQUES

The Straight-Arm Swing. The straight-arm server is usually a man, and often a power-hitter. For the beginner, this serve offers the most immediate combination of power and control. Timing the swing is easy, and if it is not a side-arm motion good height will be a benefit. Like the cricket "bowl" (pitch), a certain amount of power can be generated from the wrist and shoulder. Anyone who has seen cricket, however, can tell you that the bowl takes a lot of effort (over 10 steps) — and that it developed from a ban on bending the elbow. In tennis it is undisputed that bending the elbow to get the racket head down into the backscratcher position will increase the power and ease of the serve. Moreover, the bent elbow encourages learning a greater spin.

Most sluggers who start with a straight-arm serve quickly become dissatisfied with its relative impotence and seek advice on how to gain greater power from their efforts. Incorporating an elbow bend into the swing is always a demanding chore. Since it is difficult to feel (and sometimes difficult to believe) what is happening behind your head, a video-tape machine is a tremendous aid. For adjusting to the inevitable change in timing, patience is also a help. If incorporating the elbow bend into the swing is difficult, the straight-arm server should practice starting from the backscratcher position.

The Poke. Poking can be seen wherever there are tennis courts. A favorite serve among women, and especially older women, the poke resembles a dart throw (fig. 5 - 9). Although some power is generated from the elbow and the wrist, neither the shoulder nor the weight are used to any advantage. The ball cannot be hit down into the court or spun, but since it is generally not hit very hard, control is not a major problem.

The poke serve, like the poke ground stroke, is as hard to change as it is easy to learn. But whereas any pupil can learn, via straight-arming, to hit ground strokes comparable to the former pokes, the same is not true of serves. All the power of a serve must come from the server (a ground stroke absorbs power from the opponent's shot), and many pokers lack the strength to initiate a worthwhile straight-arm. Children under ten, who will normally gain strength and coordination, should be encouraged to serve in any fashion and from any position they can. The adult poker should practice serving from the backscratcher position described earlier.

ADVANCING THE SERVE — FINDING THE RANGE

The greatest help to someone learning to serve is to work on pitching a ball. It is important to acquire an adequate serve quickly since the serve is vital to the progress of the beginner's entire game. Actually playing is as important to learning tennis as it is to learning to play the piano, where simple pieces are used in conjunction with finger exercises and scales.

Once you are able to connect with the ball on the serve, your

Figure 5-9

first priority should be to hit the ball into your opponent's court. Aim high over the net (about three feet) and into the middle of the service box. Getting the ball into play is the cardinal rule of serving, so only after you have stopped double-faulting should you begin to experiment with placing the ball.

Placing the ball is most obviously a function of the stance and the toss. The toss, primarily, determines whether or not your ball will go over the net — if you are hitting consistently into the net, you are tossing too far out in front, and vice-versa if your balls are going so high over the net that they go out. The stance controls lateral direction — if you miss to the left when trying to hit into the right box, you probably need to stand more sideways to the net.

The pupil who stands less sideways than is suggested will usually be holding the racket with a western forehand grip. It is very common for beginners to prefer the western grip as it flattens out the serve, but this grip causes abnormal difficulties for later improvement. *Changing grips always requires painful adjustments.* If changing grips ever seems easy, there is a strong likelihood that your grip is *slipping back* during the motion. Many beginners think they are serving with an eastern grip when really the racket is slipping around toward western during the swing. Similarly the stance can deceive — some players, especially pokers, will start sideways with an eastern grip but will turn so that they are facing the net when they hit the ball with the western grip.

ADDING POWER

Service power is generated from the wrist, the elbow, and the shoulder. After these elements have begun to work for you, their efficiency will double when you learn to *lean into* the ball. Leaning into a ball is a motion borrowed from the throw. If you pitch underhand, you will step with your opposite foot while making the motion. Soft ball pitches and ground strokes make use of this timing to achieve great power. Throwing overhand demands a step forward with the right leg. When timed to the most advantage, this step forward will be only half completed at the moment of contact (fig. 5 - 10). The leg and body will then come around in what seems to be almost a fall (fig. 5 - 11). A well-balanced fall usually indicates that the server correctly timed his turn toward the net.

Figure 5-10

Figure 5-11

NET RESULTS

Pokers and westerners, as well as some other novices, will tend to bring the back foot around too soon and leave it at the base line. Bringing the foot around too late or not at all is also a beginning mistake and is often caused by tossing too far in front of the body.

Timing the fall is the key to service power. Once you are comfortable with the motion, you may desire to gain more control. When your desire and patience are strong enough, you will be ready to increase the spin on your serve.

6

For Intermediates

INTERMEDIATE STROKES

The Low Volley and Half-Volley. Since beginners do not often play net position in singles (nor in doubles either, for that matter), they are not used to moving back and forth between the base line and the net. Most beginners must concentrate so hard on just stroking the ball that they do not have time to think of strategic positioning. However as the beginner's strokes become more automatic, he starts to have time enough to wonder where he should be located on the court — to anticipate. Returning to the center of the court from the sides is a matter of course, but when his anticipation takes him up or back, as it often should, there is a good chance he will get caught between the base line and the net. In this "no man's land" where most balls bounce, he will be forced to make low volleys or half-volleys.

Low volleys must be avoided whenever possible. All the advantages of being near the net are turned into disadvantages when a ball comes to your feet and you have to volley up to your opponent(s). Low volleys cannot be angled or hit sharply because they must go up over the net, and a lob hit from close to the net could be a dangerous tactic. Low volleys can only be blocked back, and even that is a demanding chore.

To hit a low volley, you must bend your knees and meet the ball in front of you (fig. 6 - 1); a volley is more difficult to judge when it gets behind you. Keep your head down and really watch the ball until it leaves your racket, as if you were catching a grounder in baseball.

A half-volley (a ball "volleyed" just as the ball is rising from

Figure 6-1

the bounce) is to be avoided like the plague, since the ball is coming up across your strings instead of down into them.

The Lob. The lob becomes one of the most useful shots for intermediate players and should never be underestimated as an offensive weapon (especially in doubles). It takes some experience to know when a lob might be used offensively, but the defensive lob is so necessary and easily learned that it should be the first "shot" incorporated into your game after the four basic strokes. I call the lob a "shot" because it is not a new stroke but a variation on a ground stroke. Its low risk sometimes makes it an annoyingly popular tactic among women and children, whose opponents are less able to put away overheads.

The backswing for a lob is the same as for a normal ground stroke (your lob may thus be disguised from your opponents). A lob should be hit at least half as hard as a drive in order to send the ball so high that it will be tough to overhead and will give you time to get into the best position (in singles, the center of the court behind the base line). The height of the lob is controlled by the plane of your forward swing. The more you can get your racket down behind you, the more you can hit up and under the ball. Do not "brush up" on the ball, as you do on a drive. Rather, meet the ball further in front of you and impart a slight backspin (fig. 6 - 2), which will help the ball to rise and cause it to fall straighter. The use of backspin may be a new feeling on your ground strokes, but you will eventually want to master it. The feel is easily acquired through lobbing. The follow-through of the lob will bring the racket to a position above the head, with the racket face open (fig. 6 - 3).

When you are lobbing, you should think mostly of *height* — without height, depth and direction are as useless as they would be to a punt in football. When you are mis-hitting your lobs, you are probably trying to make your swings too vertical. Give your racket more chance to stay in the flight of the ball and meet it squarely. It does not take much of a vertical swing to lift the ball — some beginners do it without trying.

The Overhead. Calling the overhead a "smash" is a misnomer in nine out of ten instances. Watching professional tennis, it is easy to see where the term comes from, for the pros seem to hit overheads very hard. Remember that the pros hit almost everything hard, and do not feel compelled to try to smash.

Figure 6-2

Figure 6-3

NET RESULTS

Except on a very short ball when your opponent is at net, smashing the ball is rarely even the best option. The best "put away" is placed far enough from your opponent so that there is little chance of a lucky reflex return. Few players have the power necessary for a smash in situations where the ball would have to be bounced over the opponent's head. The pros, you should notice, will usually hit away from their opponents. Women and children definitely do not have the power to smash, so their practice time would be more wisely spent learning to hit angle overheads. Because the ball is falling down across the path of your racket, the overhead smash is one of the most difficult shots in tennis to time — more difficult than the serve. You make it even more difficult by trying to swing as hard as you can.

An overhead stroke really starts from the backscratcher service position (fig. 6 - 4). Immediately upon seeing that you must hit an overhead, draw the racket back over your shoulder the way a quarterback, preparing to pass, would draw his arm back while "dropping back" from the line. The forward swing should resemble the service as much as possible, except that the ball should be met further in front of you so that it can be hit down into the court (fig. 6 - 5). The shoulders, arm, and wrist bring the racket up over the head and follow through down by the left ankle.

The overhead is not only more difficult to time than the serve, but you must also judge the lob to position yourself under it. Always be prepared to make last second adjustments with your feet so that you can stand sideways to the net and step forward with your back foot as you hit the ball. It will aid your balance and judgement to point at the lobbed ball with your left arm, as if you were an infielder tracking a pop fly. If you "point" but are still having balance and judgement problems, minimize your swing and try only to place the ball. Do not be reluctant to let your wrist generate all the power in your shot.

When you are behind the service line, the difficulty of judging a deep lob makes it prudent to let the ball bounce. Waiting for the bounce is a good tactic on windy or sunny days. Particularly high lobs can be overheaded after the bounce, provided they do not bounce behind the service line. From more than a couple of yards behind the service line, an overhead cannot safely be hit down into the court.

Figure 6-4

Figure 6-5

The Drop Shot. Having mastered the overhead, the drop shot is the next shot you should learn. Although it is a soft shot, a "touch" shot, it is an offensive weapon and should be used only from an offensive position. There is an old maxim, "Never drop shot from the base line." Knowing when to use a drop shot and *disguising* it are as important as executing it well.

Generally the drop should be used sparingly, as a change of pace when your opponent is expecting you to force him back. The drop is a particularly effective tactic against an opponent who lags behind the base line and is slow coming up to net.

The closer you are to the net when you drop shot, the less chance you have of erring. Nothing is more likely to snatch defeat from the jaws of victory than a bad drop shot, but most bad drops are attempted from too far back in the court. The farther your drop has to travel to get over the net, the more time others will have to reach it. Surprise is the sister of disguise, not whim.

Because of the desirability of disguising your drop shots, the backswing for a drop shot should be not different from the one for a forehand or a backhand. The drop should be practiced first on a medium-paced shot hit to you. Do not push the ball or follow-through — stop your swing at the moment of impact. As you get proficient at this "stop" shot, try pulling the racket across the ball (from outside to inside) and under it at impact (figs. 6 - 6A and 6 - 6B). This cut will help in two ways. First, no matter how softly you stop the ball, it will bounce toward your opponent unless it is cut. Cutting under the ball tends to lift your shot up over the net and makes it bounce straighter up and down. A yard of margin over the net is not too much. Second, cut the drop to take some of the pace off your opponent's shot. The faster his shot is moving, the more cut you must use (and the more touch you must have).

If there is ever a time when you are forced to hit a drop shot, it is after your opponent has dropped to you. Thus the saying, "Always drop shot a drop shot." The drop shot is more valuable on a clay surface than on a hard court where the ball will bounce up too high. Any short ball on a clay court, too low to be driven or chipped, can be drop shot. Follow up your drop shot with a lob and you have a one-two combination that can make your opponent really work.

Figure 6-6A

Figure 6-6B

INTERMEDIATE SINGLES STRATEGY

Understanding a little about your opponent and the strategic concepts fundamental to the singles court will help you to play better tennis and win. In both singles and doubles, and on all levels, most points are won by errors. At the very advanced level, many errors are forced by strong shots, but it is testimony to the human competitive spirit that so many players are reluctant to concede that they could not at least have returned a shot.

Game of Errors. At most levels of play, those who are content to try for moderate shots are often rewarded. Except in very advanced play, most errors are made in attempting shots that are too difficult for the situation. *From positions which are not advantageous*, players without much experience will sometimes try to hit winners out of impatience or desperation. They would do well to remember an old saying, that "you can't hit a shot you don't have." In simple terms, if your opponent comes to net after a good shot to your weak backhand, don't swing wildly in hopes of knocking him down. The lob would probably be a more intelligent option, giving your opponent a chance to miss. Should an opponent convince you that he will not beat himself by making unnecessary errors, then you would have more reason for desperation (and impetus to practice that backhand).

Even from an advantageous position, inexperienced players will try to hit an extravagant shot — "don't try to hit a better shot than you need to hit." You will have plenty of opportunity to use the better shots you have practiced when you come up against better players. Let your opponent prove that you need to make great shots before you try them. Playing a little on the safe side will give you a good way of sizing up opponents — the "better" players will not beat themselves by erring on your safe shots.

Although no two matches can be the same, it is easy to make some generalizations about singles strategy based on the constant dimensions of the court. Getting the ball in play (preferably with the first serve) and keeping it in play are of course paramount objectives. The following rules, starting with the return of serve, will help you cut down your errors and improve your shots from common positions.

When to to Hit Crosscourt. The most vital rule of thumb in backcourt play is to hit *crosscourt*. A crosscourt ball travels over the low part of the net (the net is 6 inches lower in the middle) and goes the longest distance to the opposite base line (the hypoteneuse). While you are hitting crosscourts, your opponent would be foolish not to return to the center of the base line after each shot. If you saw him lagging to one side, a *down-the-line* would be worth a try (give your shot at least a yard of margin from the side). By returning to the center after each shot, your opponent will run as much for a series of crosscourts as he would have to run if you moved him from side to side — and he will have to change directions twice as often.

At any level of play, you will be surprised how many errors are committed by players trying needless down-the-lines. Jack Barnaby's insistence on crosscourts to all his college teams has helped produce some of the most consistent winners in Eastern college tennis. At the intermediate levels, you will want to *play your opponent's backhand*, but don't be over anxious to be the one to break a trade of crosscourts.

Starting, then, with the return of serve, the ball should be played crosscourt. When the serve is fast, do not try to take a full swing. Just push the ball *deep* crosscourt. A depth midway between the service line and the base line should keep your opponent from taking an easy offense.

When to Hit Down-the-Line. If your opponent has come to the net after his serve or at any other time, *the crosscourt strategy should be reversed*. Unless your crosscourt passing shot is sharply angled, it will pass over the center of the net within easy reach of the netman. In order to hit such an angled crosscourt passing shot, your opponent must have approached the net after an angled shot of his own. His angled approach will also leave open a better chance for you to pass him down-the-line. (Diagram 3). *Always approach the net after hitting down-the-line or down the middle.*

Other than the passing shot and the approach shot, the only other shot which should regularly be hit down-the-line is the *drop shot*. A down-the-line drop is in the air for less time and consequently gives your opponent less time to reach it. If your opponent is winning points because he is fast enough or anticipates well enough to get all of your drops, you might try an occasional

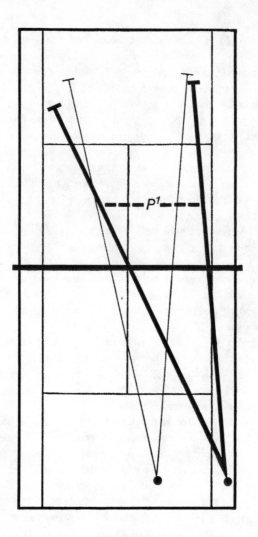

Diagram 3
THE DISADVANTAGE OF A CROSSCOURT APPROACH SHOT

crosscourt angle. This shot should be hit harder than a drop shot (with more follow-through and less margin for error over the net) so that it doesn't hang in the air too long. However, all such angles can be made more safely from the net and must be clean winners if the ball goes much beyond the sideline after the bounce, otherwise the court would be opened for your opponent to angle the ball away from you.

Always try to *aim a lob to your opponent's backhand side*, regardless of whether it means hitting down-the-line or crosscourt. Backhand overheads are weaknesses to every player except Stan Smith (his former experience in basketball seems to have given him a rare ability), whom you are not likely to play.

Moving Up and Back vs. Side to Side. Against players who do not like to play net or who are slow or apt to tire, you should be particularly aware of the up and back dimensions of singles. The singles court is seventy-eight feet long, but only twenty-seven feet wide. As long as you are near the center of the court, which is the neutral position to return to after each ground stroke in a trade, your opponent would have to play a very slim margin for error to place the ball more than ten feet to the side of you (unless he was close to the net). A good drop shot, on the other hand, could run you up twenty-five feet, and could be followed by a lob which would run you to the back fence. The more you can control the depth of your shots, the more tennis becomes an up and back game.

There is another facet to playing an up and back game — moving up and back youself. Because you can hit wider angles with more safety from the net, moving up actually opens the way to running your opponent more to the side. Another advantage to moving up is that the closer you take the ball to the net, the more you can rush your opponent.

7

Singles—The "Up And Back" Game

At the intermediate level, singles should start becoming an "up and back" game — a game whose strategies are designed primarily to exploit the length of the court rather than its width. At the end of the last chapter we discussed some reasons for this emphasis, and some players may be able to put our theory to practice. Others, however, may desire to see exactly how they should incorporate up and back strategies into their game.

The best way to improve up and back tennis is to observe players of a similar style and level of play. Although everyone's game is different — no two people can play exactly alike, even when someone tries to imitate another — the basic strokes are performed in several general intermediate styles which are easy to recognize. Another player can quickly be discovered with a similar style of stroking, be it technically correct or faulty. Learn by watching him compete against other types of players. Ask what part "up and back" play has in the winning or losing of points. For example, does the player try to move up closer to the net to hit offensively or volley? Or, does the player try to draw a particular opponent up to the net? Why, or why not?

To benefit from court-side observations, this chapter of hypothetical matchings between the common intermediate styles of play is offered. Some of these styles will be familiar after reading Chapters 2 - 5 on the basic strokes. In as much as technique usually reflects physique, physiques — and thus the ability to move — can be assigned to accompany the stroking styles in our hypothetical matchings. Most players should have no problem immediately identifying with one physique and style of play.

Each style will be played against other styles so that you can see the kinds of situations you may expect to meet. Advice will be offered on how each style could better handle other styles, tactically and technically.

Ladies First. The normal difference in physique and athletic ability between men and women is reflected in styles of play — intermediate men generally play a more aggressive, net-rushing brand of singles. Women are more apt to neglect their forecourt play in developing ground stroke drives which are stronger relative to their play. However, as there are many exceptions to the differences in physique, all stylistic variations are observable in players of each sex. (To break the monotony of reading masculine pronouns, I am using feminine pronouns throughout the rest of this chapter — even as I'm charged with "tokenism.") Although men are urged to hit deeper to keep most opponents away from the net, and women are urged to practice hitting and handling short balls, this advice is only of very general value.

The *stroker* is generally a tall girl who stands two yards or more behind the base line and waits for the ball to drop down to knee level to lift it up in her long, graceful swing. She lets the racket head droop way down rather than bend her knees. Her forehand is definitely her preferred stroke, and she likes to make it smooth and deep. A good service motion will probably be flawed by an unnecessarily high toss, which will cause errors on the first ball. The second serve will be slow. Her backhand will probably be an inconsistent slice.

The stroker will play her best against others who have similar styles. A variation on the stroker is the *hitter*. Whereas the stroker's shots will be hit to arc over the net, especially when she has to run forward, the slugger will try to hit flat, low drives from every position. She may be heavier or stronger, or she may just be impetuous. The more often her good shots (a strong forehand or perhaps a two-handed backhand) overpower her opponent, the more the hitter is playing against herself. Frequently she beats herself — the odds are discriminating when every ball is overhit. Her style is apt to be more suited to doubles, especially when men are involved. Her serve may rise to the occasion and her overhead could be a strong point. As men don't like to be overpowered by women, a hard hitting female will incite them to hit harder than they should. The hitter's best chance is always in a hitting contest.

The *hitter vs. the stroker*. Odds go to the stroker in a close match. The stroker may be slightly in awe of the hitter, but the hitter's hard shots will carry deep to the stroker's strength. The match may be close, because the hitter will be less impatient playing against the deep returns of the stroker than against shorter balls she would feel obligated to smash. In the long run, the stroker will return more balls than the hitter will be able to put away.

The stroker's nemesis will be the short ball because she stands back so far and lets the ball almost drop to the ground before hitting (a slight misjudgement and her swing is too late). One type of player who will give her many such short shots is the *poker*. The poker often takes balls while they are still high, and chops them down. The stroker is going to feel rushed and will definitely lose, unless she moves in closer; but even then she will have trouble. It is hard playing on new ground. The stroker's depth will be of little avail against a smart poker, who will volley the high arcing balls back short. Of the two players, the poker is much more comfortable at net since the blocking motion is similar to a poke. Pokers tend to be small and quick, which is an added advantage at net. Naturally they are good doubles players — unless they are overpowered.

The *hitter vs. the poker*. The hitter stands a better chance against pokers because her harder, straighter shots cannot be as easily volleyed or taken on the rise. Pushed farther back in the court, the poker will not be able to chop effectively. Also, it is hard to time a chop against a hard shot. The hitter has only to beat her opponent (and not herself). Don't blame me for leaving the outcome in serious doubt.

There are two other basic types of women players who are more difficult to predict. The *wristy* player can be versatile and effective, especially against strokers and hitters. Unlike the stroker, whose wrist may bend during a graceful swing, some players use a little wrist (and *hand*) for control. They grip the racket tightly enough to prevent it from turning, but loosely enough to let a slap generate naturally. They are usually shorter, tighter players, and the same short, slapping motion can hit an angle or a light drive. The light drive and angles can be handled by a *poker*, who is willing and able to bend her knees, so the wristy player may need a net game and a serve to compete evenly. Whereas the low backhand was the poker's weakness, the wristy player, lacking power, flounders on high backhands. Inconsistency will be her main problem.

A woman who can run, throw, and catch well, will develop a style of her own. This "athlete" will step into the ball and hit shots, often with topspin, that will be heavier than the flat shots of the hitter.

A heavy bounce will cause more trouble to the poker and the wristy player, both of whom take the ball earlier than the stroker or the hitter. The athlete will have the coordination to hit short against those who play deep, but whether she will think to do it is another matter. If she has a weakness, it is that she underestimates the efficacy of styles less athletic than her own, and is sometimes impatient to force her opponents. Other types of players can put pressure on the athletic player and force her to overextend herself, if they learn to play better from different positions further up or back.

Pokers and wristy players who wish to stand up to a stronger game must learn to play from farther back and to step into the ball more. This will add power to ground strokes which are too weak to be effective from behind the base line.

Because women have less natural affinity for net play than men, they gain less experience in the front of the court. Most intermediate women who practice a limited amount of time hit a few practice volleys in the warm-up and then retreat to the base line. Even if they try for every ball on the first bounce, they get little practice dealing with the many balls that must be hit between the service line and the base line. Strokers and hitters, especially, should rally for a while within the service boxes to gain the desperately needed experience in this area. This practice, rather than absorbing time that could have been spent warming up ground strokes, will serve just as well in getting your eye and racket on the ball. Done vigorously, it will also warm you up.

8

Practice for Intermediates

PRACTICE THAT ENCOURAGES

Practice sessions serve two functions: first to improve technique and then to encourage the use of the technique in a match. A common feeling is that the value of practice sessions may be negated by competing before a stroke is "ready," but old techniques are not further ingrained by use. Nor do they disappear by disuse. Rather, they are supplanted by strongly ingrained new techniques. Muscles master new techniques slowly, by *repetition*, but they forget the old techniques even more slowly, only with *experience*. A player will, for example, practice lengthening an aborted backhand follow-through against the backboard for fifteen mintues a day, and during the several weeks' practice he may feel he has improved — until he plays a match. During the game he may lack control or even revert to his old technique, and, of course, he will wonder why his practice has not helped. The reason, to a good extent, is that the repetition of a new technique in a practice sessions creates an artificial situation where one's concentration can be fixed on the desired improvement. Beyond a certain point, a player must practice incorporating the technique into a more realistic playing situation. The practice sessions described below in the backboard section and the net play section include methods of simulating match play situations.

Even the very gradual incorporation of new techniques into one's actual competitive game usually demands confidence. Most players need encouragement to help their confidence and play their best tennis. In addition to providing a simple structure to promote helpful repetition, the following practice sessions are designed to be encouraging and pleasurable for players of all ages and abilities.

GROUND STROKE AND SERVING TARGET PRACTICE

The basic tool of a good practice session is a target. There is something magical about having a target at which to aim, and aiming at the same spot over and over creates the repetition that grooves a swing. While better players will usually hit a given target more frequently over a period of time, the target should be just small enough to allow luck to play a significant role. Games are generally more encouraging to players of differing abilities if an element of luck is involved. Thus the trick to making target practice most enjoyable lies in choosing the best available target and in positioning it. Determined players will try for a seemingly impossible target, but others will stop concentrating unless the target is hit or changed with some frequency.

On the court. A target can be placed on either side of the net, depending on whether one or both players want to be aiming at the same time. Swings are most consistently grooved when both players hit for a single target, and a game is easily made of the contest. In any target contest you could incorporate some of the following rules:

1. The target must be hit before the bounce.
2. The ball must be hit before the second bounce.
3. No goal-tending (stopping the ball before it has a chance to hit the target).

The easiest way to score is to count each "hit" as a point, and to play a short game before moving or swapping targets.

An alternate way of scoring is to count each hit on the target as plus 25 and each error as minus 1. If only one player aims at a target, and time or the number of shots is used as a measure of the performance, conditions come closer to approximating those of a match. The contest becomes much more advanced when each player has a choice of targets to hit.

If some equalization of a target contest seems necessary, the targets can be arranged so that one player will have to aim with a stroke he finds difficult (perhaps a deep backhand). His opponent can hit with his strength (perhaps a short forehand). If targets are hit too often for your taste, they can of course be reduced in size or moved nearer the base line, which will force both players to hit from a distance further away. Progressing to the diminutive, popular targets are: chairs, large tennis ball baskets, piles of rackets or dirty clothes, tennis ball cartons, tennis racket covers, and tennis ball cans. One must be very advanced and also patient in order to hit the smaller targets. If large targets cannot be used because of the danger of damaging the court surface, or if a very large target is desired, the proper-sized area should be marked off on the court by lines or boundaries.

At the backboard. Besides being the best place to practice a stroke that is in need of constant attention, the backboard can be used for more advanced practice sessions when court space is scarce or expensive. Targets may, of course, be drawn on backboards, but when even backboard space is scarce, or when you are tired of practicing by yourself, a playing experience can be simulated. "Rotation" is a popular backboard game that can be played by two or more intermediate players (more than five is a crowd) on any backboard with a net-high line and three "out" boundaries. The players form a line either behind the court or to the side, depending on space and safety considerations. The player at the beginning of the line serves and then hurries out of the way and around to the back of the line, while the next player steps out and hits the return. And so on. The ball should be hit after the first bounce, and the player who hits the target becomes the leader. Any time a player misses the ball, he goes to the end of the line and the leader starts another rally. As the point may never get to the end of the line, there is a great advantage to being first. Whoever hits the target first, five times, wins the game.

"Rotation" is not much fun unless it is played by intermediate players, for the line should sometimes "go around" without an error. Obviously, the steadier the players, the more each can play.

There is a popular variation of "Rotation" — called "Elimination" — that includes more players. The net-high line and three "out" boundaries are needed, but not the target. The game is begun the same way, but when a player misses, he leaves the line. Finally, only one player, the winner, is left. Each rally is started by the server, the winner of the previous game. The other players join the new line in the same order they left the old one — the first player who left the old is the last to join the new line, and so on.

PRACTICE AT NET

Target practice is also a good way to improve your net game. The target is placed close to the service line in order to encourage players to keep their volleys low. Although a target can be set up for the base line player, just passing the netman will be challenge enough. The rallies should be started by the netman with a reasonable shot, and the scoring should reflect the difficulty of each player's task. If the base line player receives a point for each exchange he wins, the netman should receive fifteen points for each "hit" on the target. If the base line player scored points only on "clean" passing shots he would not be penalized for wild attempts.

A more advanced game at the net is called "Hot Pepper," absolutely the fastest way to improve a net game. "Hot Pepper" became popular when the Australian champions — superb volleyers — were observed regularly playing it. The game is played by two players (or four) starting at opposing service lines. A rally is begun with an underhand serve by one of the players, and an exchange then proceeds almost as a normal point would in regular tennis (the serve, however, must bounce in the service box). The only unusual rule is that in singles a ball cannot be hit beyond the opposing player's reach. If this happens, the point is not counted and a foul is attributed to the player who hit the ball (Three fouls bring a penalty of a point or more.) The ball cannot, of course, be netted or hit out. With four players, the alleys are designated "out" to promote long exchanges. Strategically speaking, the idea is to keep a rally going until one player hits down at his opponent and forces an error. An easy ball may be rushed and smashed at the opponent, who is within his rights to retreat if he has time.

"Hot Pepper" should train you to keep the ball low and to move in aggressively at the first opportunity — before your opponent moves in on you. Fast reactions and killer instincts are favored, though novice net players will do better to try to outsteady their opponents.

LOB AND OVERHEAD PRACTICE

The way to practice overheads and lobs is in a contest, one against the other. One player or a team starts at the service line and begins a rally, slowly, to his opponent(s) behind the base line. The player who is in back must lob every ball. A game might be played to ten and then started again, with the roles reversed.

Normally the advantage is with the player hitting overheads. When this advantage becomes too oppressive, measures should be taken to help the lobber. A few suggestions are:

1. Play two back, against one up.
2. Let the back player try any shot he wants after the opening lob.
3. Draw a line, a yard behind the service line, behind which the net player is not allowed to step.
4. Count an overhead returned as a point.

These handicaps are listed in order of their difficulty for the net-man. Other penalties and handicaps could be arranged to suit the circumstances. Doubles partners should practice up-and-back together, covering lobs and calling them for each other.

9

Match Play Theory

CONCENTRATION

Any player who has developed stroke habits and who has competed regularly knows that concentration is as much a part of tennis as execution. Recognizing the "inner game" has become the subject of a book by Timothy Gallwey. In his zeal to find Zen pleasures in tennis, Gallwey makes a big point of suggesting that players not "try too hard" — that they relax into "unconscious/consciousness." For the many players who may be suffering from tight nerves, Gallwey's advice can be valuable. It is certainly valid advice in its origin, teaching stroke production. A stroke cannot be learned by a nervous pupil, which is why strokes should not be practiced during match play or warm-ups, when you are apt to be nervous or tight.

However, styles of concentration in match play are personal and differ almost as widely as players' games. All players experience nerve problems of some sort, but for many players of all levels conquering nerves is not the most substantial victory to be achieved on court, as it seems to Gallwey. While "stage fright" is universal before a "big" match, the amateur tennis player neither acts nor performs primarily for an audience the way the amateur actor does. Conquering nerves is not usually prerequisite to concentration when the matter at hand is as relatively uncomplicated as noticing whether or not an opponent has a good backhand. Some players take longer than others to "warm-up" physically or mentally, but nerves and tightness cease to be a major problem during the exertion of a match.

During a match, play and concentration should be continuous; the only "fear" is the thought of losing a particular point. Everyone feels important points — that is what makes close tennis exciting. Frequently spectators "feel" points more strongly than players because they are less actively involved in the tactical problems of that point in the match. Players who are certain that nerves are their greatest adversary during important points — players who can say that they knew what percentage shots to play and that they erred because of nerves — should make an effort to play the game "point by point" and forget about the total score until they have gained experience. Other players may not share the problem of over-nervousness, but they may be instead a little too nonchalant on important points.

In intermediate tennis, fewer points are recognized as being important than there are in advanced tennis, where service games must be more consistently held. So the man of moderate means can and must be "penny-wise." In more advanced tennis, a player cannot hit the percentage shot every time against a thinking opponent, so he must recognize when it is key to keep the ball in play and when to take a slight chance. In short, he must recognize important points and consciously plan how he is going to take them. If his style is a bit too casual, he should not hesitate to tell himself to push particularly hard on an important point.

Though *confidence* is a boon to one's concentration, it cannot be bought or held permanently. The only way to insure it is by *experience*, as vital to good tennis as a second serve. The finals between John Newcombe and Bjorn Borg of the 1974 World Championship of Tennis is a perfect case in point. Before the match, both players were confident of victory. Only seventeen years old, Borg is noted for his coolness — he seems to have grown up without nerves. In the style recommended by Gallwey, Borg is "unconsciously/conscious," par excellence, regardless of the importance of the point. Sometimes he plays "out of his head" for long streaks without disastrous slumps in between times. During the first set of his championship match with Newcombe, it was Newcombe who was nervous, missing volleys and "choking" on returns. He made fifteen errors and only twelve winners, while a phenomenally loose Borg made twenty-four winners and only thirteen errors. Newcombe, however, is not afraid to show nerves or emotions. (Borg is an emotionless player.) His greater maturity and experience — Newcombe has thirteen years more experience than Borg — told him that his own confidence would grow and that Borg could not continue to play so well, "out of his head" or not. The result: 4 - 6, 6 - 3, 6 - 3, 6 - 2 for Newcombe.

More than any other player in the world today, Newcombe knows that the most important matches are not won by playing coolly "out of your head." His winner's attitude is universally recognized as being the result of a tough ability to assess the important points and to play them well, with all the determination and grit he possesses. In his match with Borg, each player was extended to deuce in six service games. Newcombe lost none of his games, though he faced four break points, while Borg, who fought off five break points, still lost three of his games.

Willing to recognize that even his skills and concentration have mortal limits, Newcombe is able to improve and add yearly to his tactical knowledge and experience. As Borg gains experience, learning to take some of the pace from his first serve and to add depth to his second serve, he will no doubt become a more awesome competitor. Already he seems as close as any other player — including Ilie Nastase, Jimmy Connors and Arthur Ashe — to joining the ranks of those rare tennis geniuses, Rod Laver and Lew Hoad, whose shotmaking seems to present superhuman obstacles to the toughest competitors in the sport, John Newcombe, Pancho Gonzales, and Ken Rosewall. Thus style and temperment differ at the highest levels of the game.

Jack Barnaby is always quick to point out that tennis is a "sport" and as such ranks no higher than third in the priorities of most players — behind family and work — and usually friends. It is silly to place too much importance on tennis when a mere turn of an ankle can keep a player off the courts for months. However, regardless of whether played professionally or recreationally (to relax, to exercise, to win against opponents or in the self's competition against nerves), there will be some mix of Newcombe and Borg in every competitor. Working to sort out or express this "mix" is a personal matter, bringing a variety of triumphs, pleasures, despairs and confusions.

DOUBLES STRATEGY

Playing Net — Obligation or Privilege? It may come as a surprise, but playing the net in doubles is not considered an obligation but a privilege to be earned, an advantage to be taken. Most beginning players are told to stand at the net when a partner is serving or receiving. However, a netman should move back to the base line if he is making errors or allowing winners that are causing his team to lose. You try *starting* at the net because as long as a net game is not an obvious weakness for opponents to attack, it can exert pressure on them: out of habit they may try to keep the ball away from a netman, and thus reduce their hitting area to a half of the court. If your partner is winning while you are at net, stay there. *Never change a winning game*.

Players frequently wonder exactly where they should stand when they are at net. Wondering where to "stand" is the wrong way to word the question. There are two basic *starting positions* at net, but a useful netman moves around some during every point.

Where to start when a partner is serving. When a player is serving, his partner should start only two or three yards back from the net and as far out into the middle of the court as will enable him to return, with a single giant step, the balls landing in all but the outside yard of the alley. If the serve bounces near the middle line between the service blocks, which is generally the best place to aim in doubles, this net position will give the netman sufficient protection from being passed down the alley by any reasonable return of a reasonable serve. If your partner serves wide, you must move a step toward the alley to *stay parallel to the ball*.

Stay parallel to the ball. Doubles is a game of little steps taken at the right times. In the example diagrammed (diagram 4), all the players have assumed the usual starting positions for a point served by player P[1] into the forehand service block. In court **A**, P[1] has served down the middle to P[4], who must then aim his return back to P[1]. P[2] knows P[4] has little chance of passing him down the alley with the return, so P[2] can safely step out to *poach* the crosscourt return that passes near the middle of the net.

This "poaching" is a duty and should be encouraged by the partner who could make no such offensive shot from his position further back in the court.

In court **B**, P^1 has served wide to P^4. P^2 must still stay parallel with the ball, but this time it will mean "covering" his alley rather than poaching.

Return serve crosscourt past the netman. Resist aiming the return of serve at the netman or down the alley except to make the netman "honest" if he is poaching too well or starting too far from the alley during the serve. Then, even if the shot is missed, an alley attempt may have some "scare" effect, deterring the netman from future poaching. On the other hand, miss the attempt too many times and the netman may poach more often or fake a poach, hoping to lure you into making errors.

Resist the temptation to hit to a good netman when returning. If returning serve crosscourt past the netman is a problem, try lobbing over his head. Since he must play fairly close to the net to effectively poach your return, *a deep lob can be an offensive shot.* It may at least encourage him to start further back when his partner serves. Should he leave the lob for his partner (the server) to retrieve, you will have time to start to the net before the server.

Move together as a team up and back. A team can gain the advantage in doubles by "taking the net." The side with both of its players at the net first will probably force the other side to retreat to the base line. Whenever possible, players should move together up and back from the net — the one-up - one-back position leaves a space between partners into which their opponents can safely place a winning shot from the net. It is better to force your opponents to try placing the ball toward a sideline where they might miss or open the court (diagram 5). In court **A**, player 3, P^3, has stayed at the net and therefore P^2 can make a safe winning shot in the shaded zone. In court **B**, P^3 has retreated back to the base line, allowing P^2 no such easy winner.

Where to stand when a partner receives serve. When your partner is receiving serve, start on the service line, about a yard and a half from the middle line between the service blocks. You can start closer to the net when your partner's serving because the serve is a relatively predictable stroke that cannot be interfered with by the opposing netman. (However, if his serve is predictably weak, you might be better off at the base line). From the service line you can drop back toward the base line if your partner is likely to lob or make a weak service return that would allow your op-

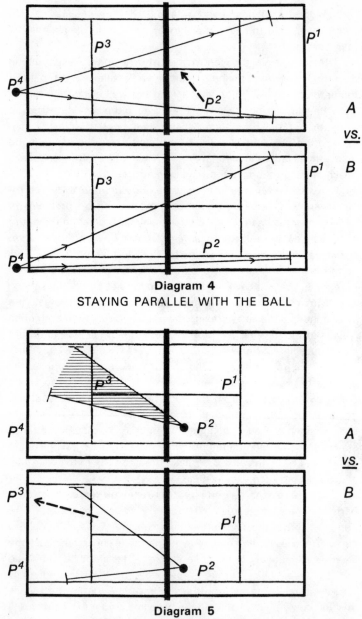

Diagram 4
STAYING PARALLEL WITH THE BALL

Diagram 5
PARALLEL MOVING, UP AND BACK

ponents to take advantage of your position at the net. If your partner makes a good return crosscourt past the opposing netman, you can move up closer to the net where you might be able to poach. Move back to the service line if you do not poach, unless you are confident that your partner will not set up either opponent. Meanwhile, the opposing netman will have moved similarly, according to the situation from his point of view. This see-saw moving up-and-back should continue until one player retreats or another player comes to net, tipping the scales.

Perhaps it is beginning to be obvious that the exercise involved in doubles almost equals that in singles. You may be hitting only a quarter of the shots, but to be in position to return them requires moving as constantly as a basketball player. If you have not been patient and confident in your movements, you will miss when finally you get your chance.

The importance of the middle. It may also be growing obvious that the middle of the court is very important in doubles. A serve can be most effective when hit down the middle because it allows the server's netman a greater chance to poach the return. The receiver usually plays the court that will put his stronger stroke in the middle where it can be of most use. Thus a right-handed player with a better forehand than a backhand will play the forehand court. Together they make an ideal team. Neither player would have to make the generally more difficult crosscourt return from the middle of the court with a backhand.

When in doubt where to place the ball, the middle is the best target zone. The ball can be hit lower and still get over the net since it is six inches lower in the middle. If a ball goes between your opponents, they may be confused as to which one of them should take it. To cut down on confusion when this happens to you, the forehand in the middle should take any shot either player might reach at the same time. Ideally, you and your partner will not be at exactly the same depth. The player closer to the net is in a more effective position and should take any balls he can reach. The last one up to net on a side will usually not come in too much closer than the service line, in order to guard for a lob.

As the majority of balls cross the net near the middle of the court in doubles, the netman who moves toward the middle the most often will get to make the most volleys — provided, of course, he does not give his opponents time to make easy shots down his alley.

The Importance of Lobbing. The importance of lobbing in doubles at all levels cannot be stressed enough. If play at net is active, a team will usually be on the offense or defense — there are fewer ground strokes traded in doubles. A lob on defense is essential if your partner needs time to retreat from the net. If you lob over an opponent's head, you may have time to go to the net and take the offense.

An effective netman will probably be playing close to the net, where of all shots hit at him from the backcourt he will be most vulnerable to a lob. He can avoid low volleys by taking them just as they come over the net, and he might make a lucky reflex volley from a drive hit hard at him to scare him from the net. The lob is the easiest and safest way to deter a player from moving in close to the net.

Unless one opponent is closing in or has a weaker overhead than his partner, *lob down the middle*. A lob down the middle may create confusion if your opponents do not work well together. Lobbing over a lone netman can be a good idea. When it happens to your team, have the player in back cross behind the netman while the netman crosses to the other side and comes back. Stay at net after your partner's lob only when confident that the opponents will not come to net and take advantage of your one-up - one-back position.

Communication Between Partners. Communication between partners is a vital aspect of play. Call "lob" if you want to tell your partner to move back, or say something more subtle to prevent opponents from understanding your intent. When your partner is receiving serve, you should call the service line so that he can concentrate entirely on hitting. Form a habit when at net of calling balls "out" to stop a partner from volleying "out" balls — most partners will quickly learn to appreciate or ignore this contribution.

During a point you should *know* where your partner is, and what shot he probably will hit. For example, will your partner try to come to net after returning the opponent's second serve, or will he stay back? If you are looking back or over to see what your partner will do, your opponents may come to net or poach and catch you by surprise, a "monkey in the middle." *You should not watch your partner while he is actually hitting the ball.* Watch your opponent's shot until you are certain where it is going (watch it bounce, if you think it might go "out" and call the line for your partner), and then look to your opponents. It will improve your anticipation to *watch the opposing netman* while your partner is hitting — since the opposing netman is watching your partner and anticipating his shot, watching the netman will tell you what both of them will do.

Part of knowing what your partner will do is knowing what any partner *should* do, but you must of course study your partner's particularities. Each player reacts differently in certain situations, depending on his strengths and weaknesses. *Discuss with your partner what each of you are inclined to do.* Part of hitting your shots with maximum confidence is knowing that your partner expects and appreciates your attempts.

A climate of openness will facilitate changing tactics or tendencies that are not proving effective. While new tactical problems often must be worked out on the court during a match, off-court preparation and compatibility can clear the air.

On court, each player should prepare for every point; not just for the ones he is serving or returning. For example, try to guess what your partner will do with his return, if a plan has not already been worked out. Often the tactical ploys of even the cagiest players can be predicted, and often opponents will ignore obvious percentage play. A lot can be learned about a person from his tennis game.

10

Match Play Analysis

THE MATCH

Techniques to improve intermediate stroking, concentration, strategic theory and situation tactics have been presented thus far, but players occasionally wish to know exactly what goes on inside other players' heads during and between consecutive points in a match. The wish is neither unreasonable nor impossible to fulfill.

A head confused by too many theories and instructions may not be able to benefit from personal experience. Vicarious experience, however, may sometimes help a player sort out his situation. Watching good or great tennis often has an exhilarating influence on one's own game, bringing improvements that seem to last. Television commentary during matches is improving in its efforts to relate to the average player, but making matches exciting can work at cross-purposes. Spectators, caught up in the excitement of matches, begin to visualize themselves playing the fantastic tennis they are watching. Later, on the court, they may be depressed as they compare their own shots with those they have just seen televized. These spectators would do well to find more realistic models for their fantasies.

Although watching intermediate tennis may not sound exciting, millions of players with average abilities find *playing* intermediate tennis exciting, even when they are not having "spectacular" days. Just observe an intermediate match closely, and stick around after a match to sense the genuine excitement. To help you understand what excites these players, I am going to guide you, point by point, through an average set between intermediate players, commenting as though I were an omniscient sportscaster.

The players have not seen each other before, so your disorientation at the beginning of the set will be only slightly greater than that of the players. When you are familiar with the general styles of the players, try to imagine yourself as the one whose style is closest to your own. This identification may help to give you insights about the specific kinds of thoughts (tactical and technical) and the range of feelings you as the player might experience from point to point in the match.

To widen the appeal of our match analysis, I have chosen to work with a set of doubles. With four players, you will have a wider variety of styles with which to identify. A "pick-up" doubles set is also apt to be more exciting because doubles tend to equalize abilities. The premium is on readiness rather than speed or strength. In singles a player must always work and run to gain offensive positioning, whereas in doubles a player starts from the offensive, at least part of the time. This start is part of the reason that many a smart old tennis veteran may still control a doubles match against younger opponents even though he can no longer compete against them in singles. The other part of the reason is tactical — playing with three other players requires more sophistication than playing with one. Although one player may start with a strong offensive position at net during his partner's serve, his position can turn immediately into a weak one, if his team does not play intelligently. The volatile nature of doubles should increase its appeal as a subject for match analysis.

We will begin the set with player *B* serving. To keep it simple, we will assume our match is indoors where neither side is adversely affected by wind or sun or background colors. Player *B* is serving first because player *B*'s partner, player *C*, guessed that *B* might have a better serve due to his superior height and strength. It is always wise to have the better server begin the set — if the set is won 6 - 3, *B* will be the only player to have served three times. After any set, the serving order of partners can be reversed to maintain this advantage.

B, who is quite big, has a hard, flat serve, but it usually takes him a while to find the range. He faults his first ball into the net, but gets his second ball in, to player *D*'s backhand. *D* has hoped to return from the forehand court for the first set because his forehand is his strongest shot. *D*, a stylist — of the four players, his form is the most perfect — is not happy with *B*'s serve to his backhand. But he does not run around it this time, since not yet knowing *B*'s serves, he isn't sure he'll have time to run around his second serve. *D* makes a flat backhand crosscourt to *B*, who has stayed back behind the base line after his second serve. *B* pushes the ball back to *D*'s forehand and starts to net. *D* hits a flat forehand to *B*, who nets it as a forehand volley. *B* was caught running into the ball, and is slightly nonplussed at his foolish approach. *D*'s partner, player *E*, congratulates him. LOVE - 15.

After netting his first serve again, *B* puts a second serve in to *E*'s forehand. *E* is the most consistent player on the court, and plays the most doubles. He is happy to play the "ad" court. He chips most of his ground strokes, and volleys well. His return is a chip that goes crosscourt short to *B*, who has to rush up from the base line to get it. *B*'s return is a set-up for *E*, who, two yards inside the service line, volleys down at *B*'s partner (player *C*) for a winner. LOVE - 30.

B is a little discouraged at this bad start and resolves not to net his first serve. It goes out instead, and his second ball is right down the middle of the box. *D* steps around it and hits a hard forehand crosscourt, which *B* pushes back short. *D* comes up and tries to stroke a winner down *C*'s alley, but nets it trying to make a flashy shot. *D* wonders why he always "chokes" on the easy ones. 15 - 30.

B finally gets a first serve in to *E*'s backhand, who barely returns it. *B* comes up and anxiously pushes the ball over the middle and out. 15 - 40.

Cannonballing a first serve in to *D*'s forehand wins *B* a point, as *D* makes too much of a swing. (Ahead 40 - 15, *D* felt confident enough of winning the game to try a winner — a reasonable assumption.) 30 - 40.

Although *B* now feels much better, he misses his first serve and poops his second ball in to *E*'s backhand. *E* is careful not to miss, and *B* attempts a lob over *D*. The effort is a bit shaky, and *D* smashes the overhead away with ease.

GAME, 1 LOVE for *D* and *E*

A bit wary of his free-hitting partner, *E* volunteers quickly to serve first. He hopes to demoralize his opponents before they can get warmed up or are brought into the match by careless play. *B* has had a discouraging first game, and *C* has only watched the balls go by.

E's serve is a consistent slice, which he likes to follow in to net. He is careful to try to serve to the backhand. *C*, who is playing the forehand court, has a good topspin forehand drive and a weaker chop backhand. His first backhand return goes into the net. 15 - LOVE.

B's ground strokes are seldom flashy but he manages to return almost everything with an even pace. *E* has plenty of time to volley *D*'s return, but misses. 15 - 15.

E again serves to *C*'s backhand, but *C* returns it, low this time. *E* volleys back to *C*'s forehand, and *C* topspins a hard drive back to *E*. *E* makes a fairly lucky volley to *B*'s feet. Caught unaware, *B* misses. 30-15.

E misses his first serve to *B*, and stays back after the second ball. *B* returns crosscourt but does not come in to net. *B* and *E* exchange a few crosscourts, but *E*'s low slices finally get to *B*'s timing, and *B* errs. *B* reminds himself to bend his knees for low balls. 40 - 15.

Confident that he can win another point from *B* (either by coming in or staying back), *E* decides to take a chance with *C*. Guessing that *C* will be anxious to run around his backhand, *E* serves him a wide forehand hoping to catch him off guard. It works.

GAME, 2 - LOVE, for *D* and *E*

C is now serving to *D*. His first serve goes in to *D*'s forehand. The return is strong and deep, but *C* is ready with his topspin forehand from behind the baseline. *C* forces *D* to err. 15 - LOVE.

Faced with a strong forehand and a big netman, *E* is worried that his partner will not survive at net unless he can return to *C*'s backhand. *E* hits wide of the alley in his attempt at a sharp crosscourt. 30 - LOVE.

C gets another first serve in, this time to D's backhand. The return is high and down the center of the court. B takes two big steps over and volleys it down the middle for a winner (confirming E's suspicions that he might be an effective netman). 40 - LOVE.

C wonders whether he should have served first. E decides not to try as hard on this point to keep the ball to C's backhand. C misses his first serve and puts a pretty easy second ball in for E to return low to C's backhand. C shovels the ball up, but D hits the high backhand volley on the wood. The ball dribbles over to C's topspin forehand, which ends the point.
GAME, 2 - 1, for D and E

D now serves to C. His first serve is flat and he errs. The second ball is also flat and represents only a small compromise in speed. C returns it with his topspin forehand, and D and C have a crosscourt exchange ending in D's error. LOVE - 15.

D gets his first serve in to B's backhand, and E is ready to poach what he expects to be a high, slow return of serve. E has anticipated correctly, but his volley at C lacks decisiveness. C is able to block it back to D, who comes in and hits a forcing shot to B's backhand. B lobs, and E steps into the middle to overhead the lob for a winner at C. 15 - 15.

E congratulates D on a point well played, and encourages him to get the first serve in to C's backhand. D obliges, and C makes a weak crosscourt return which E intercepts and places down the middle for another winner. 30 - 15.

D misses his first serve and the second ball, which is in, is returned to his backhand. D hits a crosscourt, which is going out, but B, who has come to net, volleys it at E. E has been moving back since B's strong return of serve and is able to lob the ball to C. C overheads at D, who swings for a drive instead of a lob, and errs needlessly. 30 - 30.

Discouraged with his ground strokes, D decides to go to net after his first serve. The serve is good, but C steps easily around it and hits a topspin forehand which D cannot handle as a half-volley. 30 - 40.

E gets ready to poach, but D double faults.
GAME, 2 - 2

E's suspicions have proved correct — his partner is erratic and less experienced than he — but *E* has played enough doubles to realize that he cannot win by himself. He must encourage his partner and hope to have him get his first serve in and to return with some consistency. Later in the set he may encourage him to lob on crucial points. The opponents, *E* hopes, may not be experienced enough to capitalize as much as they should on *D*'s game. Were *B* to serve another bad game, they might become distracted from what ought to be their purpose — giving *D* plenty of opportunity to miss and grow wilder. *B* cannonballs his first serve out, but *D* nets the second ball with a backhand. 15 - LOVE.

B virtually aces *E* with a first serve. 30 - LOVE.

Another first serve takes the third point from *D*. 40 - LOVE.

B and *C* are pleased. *E* sees things are not going his way, but he is determined to give his opponents a chance to miss. After *B* hits his first serve wide of an ace, *E* returns the second serve down the middle, a nasty chip just out of reach of *C*'s weak backhand volley. *B* makes a remarkably good lob over *D*'s head (perhaps thinking that *E* had followed his return to net) and follows it to net. *E* crosses behind his partner to return the lob and drives a forehand down the middle for a winner. 40 - 15.

E muses on the success of his instinct not to lob in that situation. *B*'s lob had taken him by surprise, but *E* had felt everyone was expecting him to lob in return. *B* had followed his lob to net and *D* had retreated to the base line. With his opponents hungry to hit an overhead at his partner, it had not seemed the right time to allow *B* another smash or to test *C*'s overhead. As he thinks of this, *E* decides that *C*'s overhead must be tested soon. "In fact," he thinks, "why not kill two birds with one stone and ask my partner to lob his return of serve?" *D* agrees to try it.

B's first serve to *D* is good, *D*'s lob to *C* is too low, but *C* is so surprised that he nets it. *B* is a bit angry at that missed opportunity, especially since it means he must serve to *E* again, of whom he is a little scared. *C* is a little angry with himself for having been asleep, and he doesn't dare exhort *B* to get his first serve in. It hurts to remind himself that it was his first opportunity at net during his partner's serve, and that *E* does not seem likely to give him another one. 40 - 30.

NET RESULTS

After missing his first serve, *B* reminds himself to get ready to bend for one of *E*'s slices. This conscious effort helps, but his shot still rises to *D* at the net. *D* makes a picturesque high forehand volley for a put-away. DEUCE.

D's confidence is somewhat improved, though *E* is skeptical about how long their good fortune can last. *B*'s first serve is a restrained error, but *D* misses an easy second ball to his forehand. ADVANTAGE SERVER.

B faults his first ball again. The second ball is returned to his backhand this time, and he wisely lobs to *D* again. To everyone's amazement, *D* makes a murderous overhead. *E* is amused. DEUCE.

B is beginning to think he cannot get a first serve in to *E*, and he is losing almost every point to *E* on second serves. His first serve to *D* does go in, and *D* returns it crosscourt. Taking advantage of *B*'s slow ground strokes, *E* poaches and puts the ball away down the middle. ADVANTAGE RECEIVER.

B hits a hard first serve to *E* and follows it to net. His volley of the return is strong, but *E* manages to lob it over *C*'s head. *C* goes back but does not return it.

GAME, 3 - 2, for *D* and *E*

E's first serve is carelessly shallow to *C*, who topspins it back to his feet. *E* dribbles it back, but loses the point. LOVE - 15.

E puts in a good first serve to *B*, and puts the return through *C* with a volley. 15 - 15.

E misses his first serve, and *C* runs around his backhand to topspin a forehand down-the-line for a winner off *D*'s backhand volley. 15 - 30. *C* has picked a perfect time to vary his return and take a chance. He has little to lose against a good server and much to gain if his attempt is successful — one of the next two points will gain them an ad.

While *E* serves to *B*, *C* stays back, partly because he is wary of *E*'s net game and partly because he is always more comfortable in the backcourt where he can use his forehand. *E* faults again on the first ball. *B* returns the second ball hard down the middle, perhaps thinking that *E* would follow his serve to net. Caught off guard by this power, *E* cannot get the ball crosscourt or deep. *C* comes to mid-court and topspins a forehand at *D*, who makes an unsuccessful try to return it. 15 - 40.

E gets his first serve in to *C*'s backhand, and goes to net. The return of serve is slow, but low and crosscourt. *E* plays it back to *C*'s backhand again, and *C* lobs to *D*. The lob is short, but *D* must use a backhand. *B* starts to move back as *D* hits at him, and is able to volley back at *D*. *D* hits a forehand volley hard at *C*, who tries to step around and drive a forehand back at *D*. *C* tops it too heavily, resulting in a mis-hit error. 30 - 40.

C again decides to stay back for *E*'s first serve to *B*. The first serve is to the backhand, and *B* lobs *D*. The lob is not unusually good, but *D* hits it out.

GAME, 3 - 3

E is angry that he let up and served poorly when presented such an opportunity to jump ahead by winning his serve. *C* and *B* now know that they should win by playing *D* — and that they could have been ahead 4 - 2.

C hits his first serve in to *D*, who returns crosscourt. Anxious to get in to the point, *E* tries to poach *C*'s next shot but has to stretch too far. 15 - LOVE.

C rushes net after his first serve to *E*, hoping to catch him by surprise. The tactic works. 30 - LOVE.

C misses the first serve trying to place it to *D*'s backhand. The second serve is easy, and *D* returns it with a nice crosscourt forehand. *C* hits a hard drive down *E*'s alley, hoping to surprise *E*, but *E* has smelled the shot and surprises *D* with a sharp backhand volley. 30 - 15.

C and *E* have a crosscourt exchange after the first serve. It ends with *C*'s error off his weaker backhand, but *C* now feels that he can run around his backhand in a trade with *E*. He realizes, however, that he must get a deep first serve in to keep *E* away from the net. 30 - 30.

NET RESULTS

While thinking ahead, *C* nets his first serve to *D*. *D* returns the second serve crosscourt, and *D* and *C* trade a couple of ground strokes. *E* is anxious to poach but hesitant, and *D* finally stretches his long arm across and poaches a high ball. His poach is not a put-away, but *D*'s get is right back to *B*, who pokes it right over the net for a winner. 40 - 30.

C double-faults, trying impulsively to hit even his second serve deep to *E*. Although *E* has, in a way, forced the error by taking advantage of weak second serves, *C* might not have missed the second ball if he had acted on a plan rather than an impulse. Making contingency plans for your second serve guards you against such impulses. DEUCE.

C has another impulse, but this time he has it while he is resolving to get his first serve in to *D* — before he has begun his motion. He serves wide to *D*'s forehand on a calculated risk that *D* would try an impetuous shot. Although *E*'s experienced eye has detected the intention in the way *C* surveyed the court (*E* did not feel *C* was experienced enough to fake such a look), he could not warn his partner. Half-expecting the wide serve himself, *D* attempted a doomed down-the-line winner. ADVANTAGE SERVER.

C serves his first ball in to *E*'s backhand, and *E*'s lob attempt falls short, easy prey to *B*'s overhead. *E* reminds himself to swing through his lobs, to push them, and tries to encourage his partner to make use of the lob's possibilities. He worries that his lapse will affect *D*.

GAME, 4 - 3, for *B* and *C*

D feels the pressure to get his first serve in, but cannot do as he wishes. Trying too hard he nets three in a row. *B* and *C* merely return the second serves crosscourt and blitz the net. *D* gives them a set-up, volleys an out ball, and overhits a lob. *D* is tense, wondering why his serve foresakes him in a game, but he finally manages to remember that he should toss the ball higher. At love - 40, he gets his first ball in but misses the return because he has been concentrating exclusively on his serve.

GAME, 5-3, in favor of *B* and *C*

E doubts they can break *B*'s serve a third time. *B* and *C* do not seem ripe for a let down.

D errs off *B*'s first serve, and *C* puts away *E*'s lob return. *E* curses himself for not trying to hit crosscourt. *B* misses the first serve, but comes to net on his second ball. The tactic causes *D* to overhit the baseline. *E* wins the 40 - love point from a second serve, but *D* then loses the set with a netted backhand from a first serve.

GAME AND SET, 6 - 3, for *B* and *C*

POSTMATCH ANALYSIS

Looking back on this set, each of our imaginary players will probably remember most clearly the games in which each was under the most pressure — and could exert the most control. In sets of doubles, such games are, almost inevitably, those the player served. The server of each game must normally take the lion's share of credit or blame. Even if his serve had little bearing on the winning or losing of points in that particular game, the server probably hit more balls than any other player. Five out of nine service games were lost in our set, and the loss of each one was important. Our analysis of why our set came out the way it did will focus on service games. This focus will help to put any doubles set in perspective.

B thinks that his serving poorly was responsible for most of the trouble he and player C had with his first two service games — and the set. Although his partner missed an easy overhead, which would have won B's second service game at 40 - 15, B is right. He missed 11 out of 21 first serves in the set. While a 50/50 ratio of first serves to second serves is adequate in singles, in doubles it is even more important to avoid serving a second ball than to win a few points with first serves. This is particularly true when the second serve leads directly to the loss of as many points as it did for B. E, who let up badly in his second service game (hitting his first serves too shallow or missing them), only missed 4 first serves out of 11 in the set.

B may be disappointed in his serving, but he will not manage to do any better until he changes his approach to the task and learns to modify his first serve with some spin. In the meantime, he would be wise to try to come up with a plan to win with his serve as it is during matches. It should not be up to a partner to suggest a way to help him win his serve, especially one who has never before seen him play.

Credit must be given to C for thinking of staying back at the base line during E's first serves to B. Had he thought of using a similar tactic during B's second serve to E, B's second service game might have been saved. When it occurred to him that he rather than B should have served first, C should have considered a positive way to counter-effect his partner's service problem.

However, as I said, *B*'s service game is really his own problem under these circumstances.

C may be pleased with his solid, thoughtful play and with closing the match out at 3 - 3 on his serve. Had he missed more than 4 out of 10 first serves in the set, some of the pressure exerted on his opponents by *B*'s size at the net would have been lessened. Employing and threatening to employ individual strengths is as big a part of effective teamwork as playing around individual weaknesses.

E is ashamed that he allowed his concentration to lapse during his service game after he had stolen a 3 - 2 edge. (Experience should have taught him better.) The breaks had all fallen their way. They had broken *B*'s second service game from love - 40, and *E* should have held his serve to make the score 4 - 2. With a lead that big, *B* and *C* could easily have blown another game before *E*'s last service at 5 - 4 (perhaps *D* would have played a better service game than he ended up playing at 3 - 4), giving *E* and *D* a 6 - 4 set. While feeling that in the future a set could be stolen in such a fashion, *E* is smart enough not to bet on it. *B* and *C* seemed to be learning more than *D* during the set, despite having less to learn. The odds usually go to the more evenly balanced team.

D is definitely apologetic about his play at the end of the set (from his service game at 3 - 4), but his collapse was presaged by his style. He made six winners in the set (three more than *B*, excluding serves; one more than *C*; and only one less than *E*), but he erred eighteen times and double-faulted once. *C* erred six times and double-faulted once, and *B* and *E* made only five errors. Six of *D*'s errors came after his concentration collapsed, but he still erred twice as much as the others. His errors (and his subsequent collapse) were the result of his trying to hit his shots too well.

In advanced tennis, shots can be handled with more style than at intermediate levels, but not when doing so involves the risk of the errors made by *D*. *D* is perhaps mistaken in thinking that shots must be advanced before the game can be enjoyed as a satisfactory competitive experience. This assumption is common among inexperienced players anxious to improve. Had *D* gotten in an average percentage of first serves (he got in only four out of eleven), his partner would have been free to use his good volley at net. What *D* and *E* needed in order to stay even with their opponents throughout the set was not to hit more winners (they hit four more winners than *B* and *C*), but to win *D*'s service games.

D is more discouraged than our other imaginary players, but as we have already seen the others made no more winners. *D* is perhaps blessed with a superfluity of talent. Able to make rhythmic strokes, occasionally of a very advanced nature, he may be unable to put in the requisite practice such rhythmic timing demands. Fancy strokes and shots bring only occasional rewards, even to the advanced player who works hard at them. The ready satisfaction of tennis for all players is clearly in the art of forming viable tactics for your current level of play, and part of the joy is competing in an even match.

11

Advancing From The Intermediate

CROSSING THE RUBICON

A junior boy or girl will reap the benefits of adolescent growth in the serve, for with additional height and weight the ability to serve will improve. However, a most common service pitfall must be avoided.

This pitfall is not the result of faulty techniques but a product of that common denominator, human nature. Instead of funneling service prowess toward the development of a strong and consistent second serve and a dependable first serve, players waste their efforts attempting "cannonball" first serves and neglect their second serve. Nowhere was the result of such reversed priorities more clearly illustrated than in the 1974 World Championship of Tennis between John Newcombe and Bjorn Borg in Dallas.

Both are power servers, with strong forehands and good match temperments, but thirteen years of experience and a weaker second serve separated the seventeen-year-old Borg from Newcombe. Long noted as a super server, Newcombe served only fourteen percent winners compared to Borg's twenty-two percent. In the first set, which Borg won 6 - 4, Borg was serving his first ball harder than Newcombe: an incredible thirty-five percent of Borg's first serves were winners compared to Newcombe's not unremarkable fifteen percent. However, Borg paid a high price for his brilliance — he was able to get in only forty-five percent of his first serves. Over the course of the four-set match (Newcombe won the last three sets 6 - 3, 6 - 3, 6 - 2), Borg's first serve percentage remained fairly constant, averaging forty-seven percent, while

Newcombe's averaged fifty-six percent. This difference accounted for the decisive outcome of the match.

Both players predictably followed both first and second serves to net, and both players returned almost eighty percent of the serves hit in to them, but by getting in a higher percentage of first serves, Newcombe was at net less often after his second serve and more often after his first serve. At net more after his first serves, he made up in volley winners the edge Borg held in service winners. Newcombe made fourteen errors and twenty-one winners at net compared to Borg's twelve errors and seven winners. At net less often after his relatively stronger second serves, Newcombe was not forced into volley errors. Borg missed seventeen passing shots and won with thirteen, while Newcombe missed only four and won with fourteen. Thus the pivotal factors in the match were the frequency and strength of the second serves — exactly the factors that players and commentators had predicted would be crucial. Of fifty top professionals polled before the match, only two guessed that Borg would win.

It is interesting to note Newcombe's remark after the match that Borg should take some of the pace from his first serve, if only to avoid encountering arm problems at an early age. Newcombe had watched his compatriot and doubles partner, Tony Roche, sidelined in his early twenties due to tennis elbow. The message is clear: even Bjorn Borg, who appears to defy all rules of probability with his unique strokes, would do well to work on his second serve and resist the temptation to cannonball his first serve.

Players all over the world, despite differing abilities, age, sex and build, should learn from Newcombe's remarks. It is amazing how many players, even those lacking the physical build for power serving, will mistakenly try to develop a cannonball. They should develop instead the other weapons of a good server — placement, consistency and finesse. Excessive power actually interferes with these more vital weapons.

In order to hit a better second ball consistently, one must use spin. To learn an effective spin serve, one must have a well-timed service motion and a strength that rarely appears before adolescence. To master the spin serve is to cross the rubicon between intermediate and advanced play. For adolescents, the spin serve is usually the catalyst for a more adult game — when it is no longer necessary to play defensively after the second serve, new possibilities to attack are opened.

There are two types of spin serves — the *topspin* (or "twist") and the *slice*. A "spin" serve usually denotes the more popular topspin serve. The topspin allows the serve a yard or more of margin for error over the net. After the bounce, the topspun ball "kicks up," making it more difficult to return. The service kick has a "break" (a "curve" in baseball), because it is impossible to topspin a serve without putting some sidespin on the ball. A serve hit exclusively with sidespin is known as a *slice*. While a slice does not allow any of the margin for error granted by a topspin serve, it is sometimes of value as a change of pace. The ball breaks away after the bounce and stays low.

Learning a topspin serve takes clear precedence over learning a slice. Some players, mostly women, use slice in place of topspin because it requires less twisting of the back. (A heavy "American Twist" can be bad for the back.) Despite the lack of margin for error, the slice serve can be controlled by an advanced player. However, the slice cannot be hit very hard. It is a hindrance to a good first serve, whereas a little topspin is employed by most good servers to add control to the first ball.

The Topspin Serve. Hitting a serve with topspin is a straightforward matter of making two major changes — one in the *grip* and one in the *toss* — from the common flat serve, which is hit with a forehand grip. This is not to say that one must make both of these changes at the same time. The majority of players learn the spin serve gradually, modifying the grip and the toss a little at a time. There are other players who are so adept at tossing as to find that change readily practicable. Without tampering with an eastern forehand grip, a fair amount of topspin can be put on a ball which is tossed way back over the head. The problem with this method (besides the back trouble the "twist" might cause) is that a pupil will sometimes move around under the ball to permit his usual stroke. The desire to make a successful shot is so strong that the move is unconscious. Similarly, changing the grip without changing the toss sometimes causes players to alter the toss in a "corrective" fashion. Making a large change in the grip, however, is certain to wreck havoc on any serve, no matter how the player tries to compensate by changing his toss or the position of his feet.

Topspin on a serve is the result of bringing the racket diagonally up the back of the ball. The ball is rolled down several strings, which starts it turning over. Bringing the racket up the ball with a powerful wrist flick is possible with an eastern forehand *grip*, but with a continental grip or even better, a backhand grip, it

Figure 11-1A

requires less of a twist of the wrist — and thus less chance for error. The racket is cocked in the hand by the continental grip so that the racket face is naturally at the desired angle to the ball (fig. 11 - 1A). Figure 11 - 1B shows the racket angle when the ball is held with an eastern forehand grip.

Figure 11-1B

Obviously, if the racket is to bring the strings up the back of the ball, the ball cannot be met at the very top of the swing. Therefore, the *toss* must be moved to place the ball where such "action" can happen. A toss several inches further back over the head should be enough for a beginning. Several inches to the left is also suggested, as the diagonal swing is coming across the ball, as well as up. Were the ball to drop straight from where contact with the racket begins in a topspin serve, the server would be struck in the head (a flat serve toss would drop the ball just in front of the face).

Any change of toss and grip (to produce spin) that does not cause a noticeable difference means the change was not enough. A serve with action on the ball feels very different from a flat serve. Changing to a continental grip will cause the serve to go drastically downwards and to the left of where the former serve would have gone — a first attempt that does not fall both short and wide of the net is remarkable (and suspect). Even the topspin serve has to be erratic until the player's *wrist* learns to compensate for the new grip.

You should not align your stance so that you are turned any further away from the net than is shown in fig. 11 - 1. Aim very high and to the right of the service box at first, to the top of the fence on your right, if necessary. In time you will learn to adjust to the grip automatically, and the topspin serve will consistently reward you. Like learning to ride a bicycle, a topspin serve need only be learned once.

The Slice Serve. A slice serve is hit by coming around the outside of the ball (fig. 11 - 2). In order to get the racket around the ball, the *toss* is to the right of the flat service toss. At first, players usually find this toss less awkward than the topspin toss, since the neck does not have to be bent just to see the ball. The slice serve, with its little margin for error, sacrifices reach for comfort.

To keep from cutting the ball too much, the ball should be tossed a little further to the front of the body. How far in front may depend on the grip, which does not need to be changed from the topspin or flat serve. Although the continental grip is preferred for the topspin serve, the forehand grip is better for the slice serve, because with the forehand grip the player can slice the ball further

Figure 11-2

in front of his body. Because it can be hit further in front of the body, the slice serve creates a superior angle. The possibility of meeting the ball well out in front of the body also allows the server to lean (or "fall") into the ball with ease and thus recover some of the speed that is inevitably lost by slicing any ball.

JUNIOR DEVELOPMENT

To be qualified as "advanced," a player need not have any special weapon — but on the other hand, he should have no obvious weaknesses. The attainment of at least a modified spin-serve opens the way to possessing a solid game, but having a solid game may be further defined as having the ability to handle an advanced serve with either a forehand or a backhand. An intermediate will often be unable to defend from his backhand side after his second serve.

For adolescents, new strength and reach not only enable them to improve their serves, but this growth also automatically helps to improve their other strokes. An adolescent's net game should naturally receive an even greater immediate boost than his ground strokes. A larger wrist will be able to block a harder ball, but it is not necessarily as able to control its new strength in a full ground-stroke swing. Backhand strength is frequently still lacking after physical maturity is reached and must be increased by exercise and practice. Timing and feel come more slowly than growth and strength — they come with experience.

New strength causes new habits — indeed new strokes. A child is not strong enough to topspin a ball heavily, so his stroke comes into adolescence free of any topspin deformity. Among adolescent boys there is a common tendency to become carried away with heavy topspin experimentation. Lest bad stroke habits be ingrained, adolescents, under sixteen, should work hardest on solidifying their ground strokes (See the chapter on advanced drills and depth). More offensive shots can be developed later.

DEVELOPING AN OFFENSIVE STYLE

A solid defense is rarely enough to win matches against advanced players who have a solid defense of their own. A player must learn how to create opportunities and how to take advantage of them when they come.

Taking Advantage of Opportunities. An opportunity in tennis can be most precisely defined as a short, high ball that is not quite close enough to the net to be called a "set-up" (a chance for an easy "put-away"). While a few intermediates may take advantage of such opportunities with a "pet" forehand or a precocious net game, most will not know what to do. In general, men and women learn to take advantage of these opportunities in different ways.

The value placed on being at the net strongly affects a player's game. Player *M* wants to get to the net. He takes a short ball on its rise from the bounce and quickly approaches the net. His opponent must take five steps to reach the ball. Player *W* takes more time on the same short ball from the same opponent, winding up and waiting, not taking the ball on the rise. *W*'s shot has more speed, but lands in the same spot as *M*'s, five steps away from the opponent. *W* made the shot later and from further back in the court, with the result that the ball's greater speed gets it to the opponent at the same time as *M*'s earlier, but slower shot. In terms of time, then, all things are equal. The two variables are that *M* has been able to move considerably closer to the net than *W*, and that the opponent must deal with a faster moving ball from *W* than from *M*. *M*, who likes to be at the net, was vying for position. *W*, less confident at the net, is trying to force an error by making a better shot.

The Value of the Net: Fast Court vs. Slow and Men vs. Women. The most important variable that affects a player's decision to choose *M*'s tactic or *W*'s, is the speed of the court surface. On a fast surface the ball skids when it bounces, picking up speed, whereas on a slow surface, the speed of the ball brakes at the bounce. On a slow court there is more time to make passing shots and other ground strokes, while angle volleys lose some of their sharpness and can be retrieved. Thus the advantages of being at the net is significantly reduced on a slow surface.

Typically, however, player *M* from above will be a man and player *W* will be a woman. While net play is undisputedly of value in men's tennis (relative only to the surface being played on), the value of net play is questionable for women below the professional level. The reason for the difference is purely physical: a man's longer reach enables him to cover the court better. Playing net is a matter of inches. It is no accident that some of the most aggressive players in both men's and women's tennis have been tall (Stan Smith, and Margaret Court,to name two).

"Approaching" Net — The Chip Approach. The purpose of an approach shot is twofold. First, you want to be able to follow it as close to the net as you dare to play. This means that you must do some fast moving and that your opponent must not get to the ball too soon. Second, the approach must not give your opponent an easy opportunity to hit a good drive past you.

The approach shot that can be most quickly executed on a rising ball is a chip. The downward path of the chip's swing can be directed into the path of a ball rising from its bounce, and thus such a slice is easy to time. A short swing also contributes to the quickness, balance and controlability of the chip. No advanced player can manage for long without mastering the chip approach, even though he may not always follow it to net.

After hitting a disappointing approach shot, a hasty return to the base line is still possible — provided you sense as you hit the ball that your shot is weak. Unfortunately when you are first learning the chip approach, you may not be able to feel the result before you see it. But you cannot afford to be reticent. A learner's reticence will be felt in the chip stroke, where leaning into the ball is of great importance.

The ball should be approached with the body turned sideways to the net for either a forehand or a backhand chip. The racket is poised high, about a foot over the height of the ball; it is not taken back much further than for a volley (fig. 11 - 3). Ideally the ball is met between waist and shoulder level, over the height of the net, so that the shot does not have to be lifted delicately over the net.

The chip's spin will be achieved by dragging the racket diagonally down the back and across the near side of the ball. The racket face does not have to be too open — tilting the racket face back obviously decreases your chance of connecting solidly — unless the ball being approached was heavily spun. (Fig. 11 - 4.) The follow-through of the swing will bring the racket to waist level in front of the body, the racket pointing forty-five degrees past the

Figure 11-3

Figure 11-4

Figure 11-5

net and the face very open (fig. 11 - 5). Notice that the wrist position has remained almost locked throughout the swing. Forward impetus to the shot should not be intentionally given by the wrist, but by the arm swinging from the shoulder and being pulled across the ball as the body leans toward the net.

The result of this stroke should be a sharp shot which travels low over the net and takes a low, skidding bounce a yard or two behind the service line. The shortness (and lowness) of the approach is designed to force your opponent to hit up to you at net. This design assumes that after your opponent gives you a chance to approach, he will be playing well back and will have to rush forward to "dig up" your skidding slice. All this is generally more true for a fast surface and for women's tennis, where the players tend to play further back.

In singles matches the approach should be almost always directed down-the-line, except when there is a weak stroke on one side. There are two advantages to approaching down-the-line as opposed to approaching crosscourt. First, as was shown in diagram 1 (Chapter 3), the width of the court is harder to cover when the opponent is making his passing shot from a position wide of the singles court. Second, to cover after either approach, the net rusher must move "parallel" with the ball. In other words, if you approach down-the-line, you follow to net favoring that line a little, but you must favor that line more when you approach crosscourt. Covering a crosscourt, then, means moving a greater distance after the approach shot — you must go to the net and cross to the other side of the court. You would have to be very quick, indeed, to cover your greater distance faster than your crosscourt shot covers its greater distance. And even if you could outrace your shot, you would be committed to moving so fast that changing direction in the event of a crosscourt *passing* shot would be a feat. The down-the-line approach allows you to move straight toward the net without commitment to either side; it is clearly the superior shot.

A crosscourt chip approach might be used for variety, but usually it is neither an approach nor a slice.

Remembering to come across the inside of the ball is good for your down-the-line approach. Some players further aid their aim down-the-line by using a scissors kick to remains sideways

Figure 11-6

throughout the stroke (fig. 11 - 6). The smart player will keep his approach shot to an economical minimum. A better approach shot will not help you, if you are not at the net to take advantage of it.

12

Fast Court Play

Before the tennis boom in the late sixties brought the slower play-ing indoor surfaces into prominence, there was talk about chang-ing the serving rules at the professional level in order to handicap the serve-and-volley strategy. On the fast canvas and wood courts of the indoor pro tours before the late sixties, the server held an unusual advantage. The ball skidded so quickly after the bounce as to render ground-stroking very difficult. The server always followed his serve to net, and if the point was not won with the first serve, the first volley was apt to be lethal. While the new indoor surfaces are slower, they still favor the serve-and-volleyer, and the talk of changing the rules of serving has brought about occasional in-novations in scoring.

The grass surfaces on which the major outdoor champion-ships take place also have been criticized for similar reasons. The famous Longwood Cricket Club in Boston, host to the U.S. Professional Championships, has changed its tournament surface from grass to Uni-turf, and is now changing to clay; the Westside Tennis Club in Forest Hills, where the U.S. Open Championships are held, is also changing from grass to clay. On a clay surface not even the best serve-and-volleyers can rely solely on strategy. The result, everyone agrees, is longer rallies and more interesting ten-nis.

For the average player, however, the popularity of outdoor all-weather surfaces, paved and maintenance-free, will continue to encourage serve-and-volley singles. Even on a slow surface, following one's first serve to net is a valuable change of pace that no good player, man or woman, can afford to ignore.

But following one's serve to net is a practice that requires much experience. This chapter will describe in detail all the aspects of serve-and-volley singles, including how to defend one's self against an effective serve-and-volley attack. While most of what will be discussed is equally applicable to doubles, it should be kept in mind that doubles is not dependent on a good first serve. Because of the importance of the serve in singles, effective serving will be the first topic considered.

EFFECTIVE SERVING

Any serve has three main variables — depth, pace and placement. To keep a receiver off balance, a server must imaginatively use every method at his disposal.

Depth. Hitting the first serve into the last one and one-half yards of the service block should be every server's constant concern, whether or not he plans to follow it to net. A fast paced ball must be extraordinarily well placed to be effective if it lacks depth. A second serve should also be within two yards of the service line, if only to prevent the receiver from coming to net after the return. One must have great faith in the depth of a second serve to dare follow it to net.

Pace. A deep serve need not be a fast serve. A good server will experiment widely with his pace. On any given day, an opponent's timing might be "off" for a certain return he likes to try. Often as not, timing will be "off" where more time is given — the receiver may try to be too ambitious with a slow or mediocre service. (Don't try this tactic on a game point, and never try it twice in a single game.)

An obvious reason for varying the pace of the first serve is that any receiver may become very competent when dealing with a constant pace. Also, changing paces frees the server from the burden of trying to hit his hardest, most strenuous serve all the time. Against a player who likes to return from well behind the base line, the slower serve will allow the server more time to close in on the net.

Placement. A big change of pace is usually most successful if it is accompanied by a change of placement. The smart server will observe the reactions of a receiver, hoping to find out whether he prefers to be crowded or whether he prefers to stretch. Large players naturally have more difficulty getting out of the way of the ball, but their reach is longer. Against a fast receiver, the server must use his intuition, placing several balls right at the body before trying an angle, or vice-versa. Intuition can play a part in deciding at what point in the game to break the pattern.

As a target, the body represents a safer zone than a placement near a sideline. An accidental variation to one side or the other will not put the ball out of court. However, the farther back in the court the receiver likes to stand, the further he will have to run to retrieve an angle. Although he will have more time to step out of the way, the extra time will not be sufficient for an extra step chasing after the ball.

Stance. As can be seen from diagram 6, there is no advantage in the server changing service stance positions from "1" to "2" unless the receiver neglects to compensate by moving his stance in the opposite direction. The alert receiver gains a momentary edge if the server hits wide from the second position — a passing return to either side will have a greater distance to travel before crossing a boundary. Thus the return can be a harder one with less chance of the ball going out. To cover for the new down-the-line angle created by his wide serve, the server must approach the net closer to the line — on the far side of the court from position "2." The greater distance he must travel across the court to cover the line after the serve will prevent him from getting in as close to the net as he could from position "1." With more chance of receiving a return at his feet, the server's first volleying position is weakened.

Even so, a change of stance can be a viable option under several circumstances. A particular serve may be improved by moving or altering the footwork a little. If a serve is hit well enough into one of the "ace" zones (diagram 7) on a fast court, it may not matter that the receiver expected it. (Most serve-and-volleyers do not go to net after serving a wide ball from the right half of the court — if the ball is not an ace, they are better off staying back.) Serving from the left court, the right-handed player can better hit the middle ace zone by standing as close to the center stub as possible. This position may be adopted permanently, but most players seem to feel more comfortable a couple of feet to the left, where it is easier to serve to a right-handed receiver's backhand.

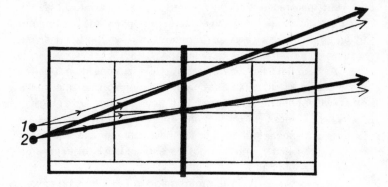

Diagram 6
VARYING THE SERVER'S POSITION

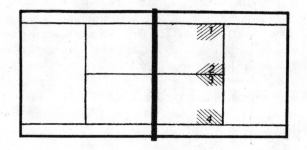

Diagram 7
ACE ZONES FOR SERVICE

Spin. To a certain degree, spin may be an important variable, apart from its function in changing pace. On high-bouncing courts against short players, a heavily topspun serve is a logical choice. On grass, a slice can keep the ball so low as to be annoying to many players.

ANTICIPATING FOR THE FIRST VOLLEY

All attempts by the server to vary his serve must be geared towards earning an easier first volley. On his best days, a good server may win points outright with his first serve, but he will still have to handle a far greater number of first volleys.

The first volley should not be depended upon to win points, even on a very fast surface. Excellent concentration is demanded in placing a volley when one is moving quickly toward the net. Rod Laver says he thinks hard about the first volley *before* he serves, since it is only before the serve that there is time to prepare. By knowing an opponent's game, and knowing how and where a return may be hit most reasonably from a certain serve, much can be done to anticipate the first volley before the point is started.

Good players often think beyond the first volley. A server may plan to close in slowly after his first volley, because he is wary of a lob. A receiver having trouble with his down-the-line passing shots may decide to lob on the first opportunity after the return.

A serve-and-volleyer cannot commit himself to favoring one side of the court for the return. As his opponent is about to hit, the server must pause on his way to the net in order to be ready to go in either direction. Most servers try to get about a yard or two behind the service line before pausing, but the distance is always dependent on the variables of serving and returning that affect the server's time. Obviously speed is a help to the server as is a service motion that encourages a straight-forward progress toward the net.

STREAMLINING THE SERVE

The most important thing to remember in serve-and-volley rushing is that a straight line is always the fastest distance between two spots on a tennis court. A service motion that leaves the server veering to the left or right should be straightened. Players experimenting with a heavy twist-serve will often find themselves falling to the left after the motion.

In general, economizing on service motion is a good idea. Any excess movements tend to put the serve off balance and slow you down. Pancho Gonzales was perfectly aligned throughout his serve and net rush, which certainly contributed toward his speed and success. Players best noted for their doubles usually show a remarkable economy in service motion, which allows them to control the first ball and follow it quickly to net. William Talbert, who was probably the greatest U.S. doubles player and theoretician, had a compact motion which popularized a serve with virtually no backswing. While the "big serve" is an American invention, a big swing is associated with European players who grew up on slow clay courts and were not as accustomed to the throwing motion.

MAKING THE FIRST VOLLEY

The momentum of a net rush gives the first volley so much power that it obviates the need for swing. After pausing to see where the receiver is hitting, the rusher moves into position and pauses again, if he has time. Ideally, he will volley the ball to where his opponent isn't, and step in as close to the net as he dares.

A good volleyer is hungry, always anticipating another shot. He must love the rapid exchange and be confident that he can win as many as he loses. His advantage, he knows, is the demand put to the receiver to achieve just in order to get into an exchange. After a good first serve on a fast court, the first volley need not be tricky — a deliberate aim may suffice, regardless of the opponent's foreknowledge of the placement. One should not, however, always aim for a corner. Against a player who returns from deep in the court, a short slice is a more intelligent shot.

If there is any little trick that will help your volleying, it is to think about holding the racket way out in front of the body. After the serve, volleys are frequently missed because the racket "disappeared" on the way to the net. Also during a fast exchange the racket may get "stuck" on one side of the body.

RETURNING SERVE

Returning serve is the most difficult part of the game. Against a serve-and-volley game the receiver must make a quick decision to try to take the offense or to remain defensive — there can be no trading shots, no middle ground, unless the server stays back. In order to decide quickly, the receiver must anticipate the server's aim, standing ready to move where he thinks the serve will probably be hit. Getting the ball in play, however, is still the cardinal rule. In the Newcombe - Borg championship match neither player missed more than one out of five serves he could get his racket on.

THINGS TO WATCH FOR IN A SERVER

Are his serves consistently deep? If not, you should be especially ready to step in to return short serves either to his feet or just beside him. Against a deep server you should first try moving back a step to give yourself more time. This will test his angle serves, but you will have time to try driving the ball well. If this is not successful in the first game, do not give up, but try alternating the tactic with moving up again or taking the ball on the rise. (Change can sometimes arouse sluggish timing.)

Does he serve to all corners equally well? If not, you might draw him into trying to place the ball in his bad corner by making it look particularly vulnerable.

Does he change the pace of his first serve intentionally? Some players only change the pace of their serve when the receiver changes his ready position. Against such a server, the receiver is wise to wait until the service motion has begun before taking a step up or back. It is hard for a server to change his pace in the middle of a swing. There is almost always a tip-off in the beginning of a motion or in the stance that will reveal the kind of serve being attempted — flat, twist, slice, or angle?

Does he ease up or bear down on important points? Sometimes the stance and motion will be well disguised and then only a knowledge of the server will help.

NET RESULTS

Does he follow every first serve to net? If not, you might be able to ascertain quickly the serves he likes to follow to the net. For example, I mentioned earlier in the chapter that many servers do not follow a wide angled serve to net. Other players may tend to stay back after hard serves because they prefer to approach more slowly, or because they do not deem an approach to the net necessary. Considerable pressure can be removed from the receiver if he does not have to worry about his opponent's net rush.

How close to the net does the server get before making his first volley? If he gets in to the service line and you can't force him to hit a half-volley or a difficult low volley, you will probably be better off trying to pass him.

Is he overly cautious with the first volley, or impatient? If overly cautious, he is giving you a chance on the next shot, so there is no reason for you to take a chance on the return. If overly impatient, play a waiting game, mixing your returns until impatience causes an error.

Has he started the match playing his hardest? If not, you should force him early when he doesn't expect it. The only time you might afford to let your opponent win an easy game is when you *know* that he will burn out — or that you will burn out.

Does he always try to serve his second ball to your backhand? If so, you might occasionally "run around" and use a forehand, especially in the forehand court. Running around makes less sense in the backhand side because it puts you out of position. It is more difficult for right-handed players to serve a second serve to the forehand of right-handed receivers, so the "run-around" can force your opponent to double-fault trying a non-percentage shot.

Is his second serve deep? Bad depth grants the receiver more opportunity to force.

Is the serve high-bouncing? A high-bouncing serve which is not deep can be chipped, sliced, or driven as offensively as a lower bouncing serve.

Does he ever follow the second serve to net? If so, watch for predictable habits. The serve that signals the start of a race to the net may begin more energetically. Try hard to give the server trouble by moving in or making a passing shot, but don't try anything rash in the hope of humiliating him. You will be better off having him feel falsely confident that he can win a crucial point when he needs it by charging the net on a second serve, than by having him think the tactic will usually excite you to try for rash winners. In the first case you will anticipate that the crucial point is to begin and will be able to prepare especially well, whereas in the second case, your rash attempts may give him too many points. The principle can be stated quite simply: don't play a poor percentage because your opponent played one first. Trying to return a second serve with a winner is generally no safer a bet than rushing net after a second serve. The same return you would try from a first serve can improve significantly on the second ball.

Where to Return — and How. In general, the return of serve should be hit to the server's feet, if he is rushing net. You can make such a return consistently, as the ball will pass over the low part of the net and will not land near any lines. A first volley cannot easily be angled from the middle of the court, especially if it must be hit up.

This return of serve can either be *sliced* or heavily *topspun.* Of the two, the slice requires less swing and is thus more dependable. A slice return is hit with as little swing as possible, almost as little as the approach shot. With the racket face open, the racket is drawn back above the height of the ball, as in fig. 12 - 1*A*. The strings must be brought down and across the back and inside of the ball, which is met a little further forward than for a drive. A turn of the shoulders toward the net during the swing will help to create the "slice," besides adding power to a short, tight swing. The wrist is almost locked throughout the motion in a forty-five degree angle to the arm (fig. 12 - 1*B*). At the end of the follow-through, the body above the hips has turned toward the net, and the racket face is open almost to the point of being parallel to the ground (fig. 12 - 1*C*).

While a slice is perhaps the staple return of most good players, topspin returns should be thrown in for balance. A heavy

Figure 12-1A

Figure 12-1B

Figure 12-1C

topspin will drop the ball at an opponent's feet or take it sharply crsscourt. A slightly flatter drive may be used for down-the-line returns. Of all these strokes, the heavily topspun one is usually the most difficult to time — the racket must cross the path of the ball unless the receiver has moved back so far as to be able to meet the ball when it is falling from the height of its bounce. A ball taken on the rise is coming up into the path of the racket's slice swing, which facilitates the stroke. The "flat" down-the-line is the best passing return, but is too hard to control for consistent use — not only is depth a problem, but a flat down-the-line that strays into the server's reach is apt to be easy fodder.

Numbers are Important. Serving or returning serve-and-volley, the server's advantage must be measured. It is not enough to know that you are winning or losing a game — the edge is never more than four points. A single silly error (perhaps due to the wind or a jolt in concentration) or a great shot by your opponent, and suddenly you are faced with break points on your serve. A player may have lost his opponent's serve three straight times without winning a point, but if he knows, for example, that the server hit eleven out of his twelve first serves in, he need not despair of getting a better opportunity to break serve. Instead, the player who is aware of the numbers will get psyched for his "number" to come up. Also, he will know when it has passed — and that it sometimes comes again before it is deserved.

In other words, by knowing the odds a player can hope to win without bearing uncalculated risks. The tough player will not mind being beaten a few times if he has played the best odds and not tried for miracles. Even some of the best players, however, are guilty of taking terrible risks. For example, Stan Smith attempted to ace John Newcombe with a second serve on match point in the 1973 Davis Cup finals. He double-faulted the match away, and the U.S. lost the cup 5 - 0. Smith admitted after the match that although he was "conservative in life," he tended to gamble on the tennis court. Some wild risks are justifiable, for instance, when a player is run way off the court by an opponent who is at net and possesses a solid overhead. But the risk Smith took was untenable and is therefore shameful. Even if he had made the ace, he stood to gain no more than a brief reprieve against a tough player like Newcombe. Newcombe would have disdained Smith's taking the risk, probably with his customary smile. No two matches are the same, but the "numbers" hardly need to fluctuate to change the outcome of a match. Most fluctuation is due to an opponent's efforts, conscious or unconscious. A player who blames his fate on good and bad days will usually find himself having a lot of bad days. Tough players however, win on their bad days, and are not likely to be tempted into trying risky, spectacular shots even when they feel great.

13

Slow Court Play

Rushing net to win the point is the key to fast court play, but slow court singles is an altogether different game. The shots vital to fast court attack — the serve, the chip approach, and the net game — are of secondary importance in this game where no serve is strong enough to guarantee a ticket to the net, and no player is quick enough to cover as much of the net after a first volley or an approach. In slow court play, the *deep drive* and its necessary complement, the *drop shot*, replace the importance of the strokes described in the previous chapter.

Mixing deep shots and drops requires touch and *finesse*, but even an effective slow court attack will not produce as many winning shots as serve-and-volley on a fast surface. If one player works himself to the net — where the angles are greater and consequently the chances for hitting clean winners — the slowness of the surface still makes it easier for his opponent to retrieve angle volleys that might have been winners on a fast-surface. Working to the net requires so many more shots on a slow court that the chance for error increases on the way.

Although more points are lost on errors in slow court play, most spectators prefer to watch the longer rallies the court encourages. Here it is possible for both players to *trade* deep drives. Normally, however, players do not trade with their very deepest shots on a slow surface any more than servers hit their hardest balls every time on a fast surface. Sometimes they trade strokes which are just deep enough to prevent the opponent from launching an easy attack. Heavy crosscourt topspins and slices provide the safest margin for error in trading, but they are difficult to handle for reasons we will be discussing.

NET RESULTS

When playing on a slow court, the receiver should try to return the serve crosscourt, in seven out of ten cases. Outside of changing his return for variety, he should rarely attempt to drive a ball very deep from a weak second serve, since the server's position, from the middle of the court, enables him to cover most of the court. As long as each player is able to get back to that middle position before his opponent hits his shot, trading is likely. Good points on slow surfaces should be comparable to tugs-of-war. Sometimes a player manipulates his opponent to put him off balance or out of court, and the player can then make a winning shot or come to net. Other times he will err trying for a good shot. In a point that involves long trading, the player who can resist going for the first non-percentage down-the-line shot will often collect the point.

Depth is the absolute measure of a good slow court serve. Spin will make depth even more effective, and it is a valuable asset. Placement assumes defensive importance; it is used to prevent your opponent from grooving his swing to your depth. A deep, spinning serve will elicit at least a few weak returns. Changing the pace of your first serve also adds a positive value to starting the point — receivers usually have plenty of time on a slow court, but they must always be made to think what stroke is allowed in their time. Learning to time the many strokes made possible by playing on a slow court is as difficult as developing and maintaining a netman's reflexes for fast court play.

TIME AND TIMING

Players have so much time for their shots on a very slow surface like clay that some develop an entirely defensive style of play. They aim only to retrieve the ball and to send it back as deep as they can. Most players must go through such a stage while they are working on their depth or gaining strength necessary for offensive play. This "pushing," as the style of play is known, often invites disdain — especially from those who are victimized by it. However, pushing is a valuable tactic to fall back on when you are unable to mount an offensive. If you are fleet of foot, at least you will be tough to beat while you hope for your timing to return. Some pushers go on to develop exceptional drives and become formidable backcourt players.

You will undoubtedly run up against troublesome pushers if you compete much on slow courts. Obviously you must *practice* forcing errors out of such an opponent so that you do not beat yourself. Forcing a pusher is actually easier than trying to force a player who pressures you to make a slip. You need only fear yourself.

Since the pusher is surviving on the time the court surface gives him, it is logical that beating him demands robbing him of some of that time. On a slow court, one way you can deprive an opponent of time is by hitting the ball sooner when you have the "opportunity." To drive or drop most effectively, *take the ball before it drops* from the top of its bounce.

Taking the ball when it reaches the top of its bounce, you will remember, was basic to the chip approach shot and slice return of serve to fast court play. To wait for the ball and try a drive offered a viable option only for those unhappy at the net. On a slow surface, where the value of being at net is never so high, a drive becomes as viable as a chip approach, except against players who have trouble running up to get a chipped ball.

Waiting for an opportune ball to drop from the height of its bounce gives your opponent too much time, and it forces you to decrease the pace of a drive to allow for the lower trajectory. A ball at the top of its bounce offers the best trajectory, and it can be reasonably timed for any sort of drive (topspin, slice, or flat). Of course, taking the ball on the rise presents greater timing and trajectory problems, especially for drives.

Although you cannot brush up on a high ball, a helpful topspin can be attained by closing the racket face and swinging straight through (fig. 13 - 1). The swing should start three-quarters of the way back and have a long follow-through. If the opponent's ball is heavily topspun, the ball will tend to ricochet off your racket strings. If the closed angle of the racket face is increased it will send the ball straighter over the net. An even more closed racket face will reverse the spin to a topspin of your own.

Reversing a heavy topspin is tricky when you are taking the ball on the rise; not only is the ball rising into the racket, but the lower trajectory for your shot demands that you hit up on it. With the flight of your racket and the flight of the ball intersecting so briefly, there is too much chance for error. The same principle

Figure 13-1

holds for slicing a ball that is coming down from the height of its bounce. Although a bounce removes most of the slice from a ball, a sliced ball is still difficult to drive because it stays low. A player who uses a lot of heavy topspin or slice may be a formidable opponent on a slow court, provided he can flatten his strokes out to make passing shots and offensive drives. Opportunities to be offensive may come few and far between against such players.

As we saw in the last chapter, after a player learns to control his serves and volleys, there is much sophisticated thinking which must be done to make his attack effective. Likewise, combatting a strong serve-and-volley attack demands quick thought and execution. In slow court singles, a finesse of a different kind is involved — a player's *strokes must be designed to feature disguise rather than economy*.

FINESSE

No matter how much you rush your shots or how hard you hit them, there will be time for an opponent to recover on a slow court. Overcoming a tough opponent on a slow court is partly a matter of attrition, wearing him down through a long match (all players begin to err when they tire). An opponent will also be worn out, mentally as well as physically, if you can *surprise* him with placements. He will have to run faster and make tiresome changes in direction when he anticipates you incorrectly. The key to surprise is *disguise*.

Disguising a shot need not involve a fake. An excess movement made to fake your opponent requires deliberation that can interrupt your concentrating on the ball and cause you to miss. It can also take time, which you do not always have when disguise is desired. The best disguise is a *constant* backswing.

The Backswing. A good backswing will look the same for a variety of different shots, thus disguising each. To hit chips, slices and drop shots the racket begins the forward motion at a level higher than the ball; and to hit topspin drives, at a level lower than the ball. Before hitting slices and drop shots, players with straight backswings must lift the racket — giving away their intention. As a drop shot demands more disguise than any other shot (when a drop shot is anticipated or poorly executed, you are likely to lose the point), the straight backswing is disadvantageous. A backswing that starts back higher, perhaps shoulder high, takes advantage of a common habit — that of *pausing with the racket about halfway back*. While this pause is not recommended for any but advanced players, it does promote disguise. From shoulder high the racket is easily brought back, down, and through in a loop for a topspin drive.

In order to prevent the racket face from opening or closing prematurely in the backswing (a tell-tale sign of a player's intended stroke), the left hand should be used to take the racket head back flat (halfway back on the forehand and all the way back and down on the backhand). This action also starts the shoulders turning sideways to the net. Open shoulders sometimes reveal an intention to hit crosscourt. For disguise, the shoulders should be held sideways as long as possible, as should the feet. A crosscourt shot can be better hit, and thus better "faked," with closed shoulders than a down-the-line can be hit with open shoulders (not enough follow-through is possible).

The fast court player should stress disguising his service backswing and stance, while the slow court player should work toward that goal after his ground strokes are disguised. Every player would like to be able to adapt his game to the surface he is playing on at the time, but most players will always have an inclination toward one or the other surface.

SPECIAL SHOTS AND MOVES

The Topspin Backhand. One good shot which often separates the good players from the very good is the *topspin backhand*. After the player has mastered the backhand drive, which has a little topspin on it, and slice backhand, he is ready to learn a heavier topspin for crosscourt angles and approach drives. To generate power for the topspin on a backhand requires using the *wrist* for power, even if it means breaking a cardinal rule of ground stroking. To a certain extent, the wrist can be turned over (closing the racket face) before the forward motion in a topspin backhand, reducing the amount of wrist flick necessary at the moment of impact. Flicking the racket up the back and around the outside of the ball demands excellent timing and a very strong

Figure 13-2

wrist. A long swing helps to generate some of the power needed and the player should further aid his effort by lifting up with his shoulder at the moment of impact. Many players actually jump during the shot. The racket ends the follow-through very high and with the racket head turned over (fig. 13 - 2).

If timed a fraction off, the topspin backhand can be a wild shot. At first, try it only when you have a lot of time to get set. Returning serve, for instance, is a bad time to experiment unless you know you are going to receive a slow serve to the backhand. The topspin backhand is also much easier to employ on balls which have fallen from the top of their bounce. Practicing ten minutes a day on the backboard is the best way to increase your strength and ability to hit topspin backhands quickly from varying positions.

The Topspin Lob. A topspin backhand without a wrist flick over the ball is apt to become an accidental *topspin lob*. The flick over helps send the ball off the racket in a horizontal path.

The topspin lob is the "boast" of good tennis; a good topspin lob is almost impossible to foresee or retrieve. The trajectory of the shot is low for a lob, because topspin cannot be applied when hitting the ball as straight up as a defensive lob. The ball should go just over the netman's reach before it drops and takes off toward the back fence. The shot has so little margin for error and requires so much feel, that at least half of all attempts probably result in errors even at the professional level. Unlike the underspin lob, it is safer to hit the topspin lob on the low side of any margin. The topspin is hit hard enough and drops fast enough to disturb an opponent's overhead. One must be very experienced before daring the shot. On a fast court the topspin lob is unnecessary — your opponent will have enough trouble getting to a lob over his head.

The Reverse Spin Overhead. On a slow court and against such weapons as the topspin lob, a player's overhead must be sharper than on a fast surface, where almost any decently paced and placed overhead will be a winner. Since the wrist is used in an overhead anyway, it may be readily employed as a means of deception.

Practice hitting overheads to both sides of the court from a similar stance. Despite what was said in the introduction to the overhead about keeping the feet aligned with the intended aim, it is possible with good timing and positioning to ignore the importance of an aligned stance. Use the wrist to direct the stroke to the "opposite" side. (Figs. 13 - 3A and 13 - 3B.) This motion, which applies a *reverse spin* to the ball, is easily camouflaged. "Pulling" the ball to get it to the other side, where your opponent will probably expect you to aim, is actually harder for some players.

The Fake. Anticipating the aim of a good overhead may be your only chance to return it, so try to discover where your opponent likes to aim them. Watch him in the warm ups — most players are more accurate hitting in one direction than in another, and a few can only hit one way.

Once you know his preferences, mere anticipation may not be enough. In that case, try a *body fake* to see if you can influence his aim. There is no secret to good faking, except that it should not be done half-heartedly or abashedly. It is as legal as it is in basketball, although not so integral to tennis.

Wait until your opponent has almost begun his forward swing, and then take a half-step in the direction you do not want him to hit. Do not fake until you have had a chance to see his preferences or habits, for then you will know better which side to fake to and what effect the fake has had. If your fake has been properly timed, you will be taking advantage of the fact that your opponent can only peripherally see you as he is watching the ball. The fake must be timed exactly; early enough and noticeable enough to draw his eye to your movement, but late enough so that he can't check out your fake without taking his eye off the ball at a crucial time (and err). Players who will not be faked can be prematurely anticipated.

On the other hand, if a player is giving you trouble with his fakes, don't let trying to outguess him distract you. Rather, make up your mind to hit three overheads to one spot, followed by two to another spot, etc. By sticking to your plan you may hit a few right to him, but since he will not be able to preguess your random sequence, he may distract himself trying new fakes.

Faking is not limited to countering overheads. A player is sometimes forced to wait in a position, more often on a slow court, while his opponent winds up to hit. A fake is most useful when you lack enough time to cover the whole width of the court but have the time to start to one side or to the other from the middle. Your

Figure 13-3A

Figure 13-3B

record will suffer if you cry wolf too often, for your opponent may ignore your fake when you most want it to work.

Especially against a player who disguises his intentions well, you must learn to anticipate his shot by *watching his racket* during the forward motion. You will be able to tell quickly where the ball is going by watching the racket rather than the ball, which is always coming in your general direction.

The Drop Volley. A wrist flick is necessary for other advanced shots, both offensive and defensive. You may remember that the wrist is turned under the ball in a drop shot. In a *drop volley,* which is usually made off a ball of good pace, the wrist turns under without going through. The wrist almost seems to pull back at the moment of impact while the arm carries through, as happens when catching a ball with a lacrosse stick. Because of this motion, the drop valley is also known as the "stop volley." You stop the ball from traveling more than a couple of yards off your racket.

When the ball has gotten behind you or is too far away for any swing or volley, a wrist flick is your desperation measure. The more advanced a player grows, the more the wrist will, almost unconsciously, become a part of his entire game.

14

Advanced Drills

The need of an advanced player for practice sessions is sometimes as basic as that of a far less skilled player. The various swings he uses in different situations go hot and cold from time to time. While he may quickly be able to straighten out or add fine points to his strokes, any new technique will be effectively incorporated into his game only after considerable experience has taught him when to use it. He also may have to choose from among several possible shots in a given situation. The drills in this chapter will help fill the need for experience and will offer as well a chance to groove the strokes and to maintain or improve the reactions, footwork and positioning.

APPROACH/PASSING SHOT DRILLS

This drill is best played by three or five players, the odd player being a useful starter and substitute. All players start at the base line, and the starter tosses a ball from the netpost which should land on or near the service line. The toss is fairly slow and high, and the player on that side of the court comes up and hits an approach shot or a mid-court drive (depending on the surface — see Chapters 11 and 12). The point is played out normally, and the approacher is given more tosses until one side has won a ten-point game. Roles should then be reversed. If the approacher wins easily, as he should, then the scores can be added up cumulatively to select a winner.

With two players on each side, the drill is good for teamwork. Only the approaching player need start at the base line — the positions of the other players can vary (either being established before the game or changed within the game by team strategy). In this way players learn what shots and movements they should try with that partner and those opponents. For example, when one player is approaching against a one-up - one-back formation, he will want to test the advantages of approaching to the player at the base line. Other tactics remain constant despite the opposition. If the approacher's partner is at the base line, this partner would want to be rushing to net ahead of the approach shot. Against two players at the base line, your approach should be made down-the-line or down the middle so that your partner can position himself in the center at the net, without worrying about covering his side of the court. Against two players at net, a hard low drive or topspin, or an offensive lob, would be in order.

DEPTH DRILLS

The only way to improve your depth is to play in a situation where you have to hit deep every time. The best way to simulate this experience is to make the front of the court out of bounds. Start playing games where any ball, after the serve, is out if it lands in the service block. Artificial lines drawn deeper than the original ones can make the game more challenging. If you have trouble improving your depth, try thinking of the path your ball must travel and how high it must be to go over the net.

Service Depth. Draw a line across the service blocks a yard and a half in front of the service line, and divide each box into three zones four or five feet wide. In a first serve - second serve sequence, serve twenty balls in a row to each of the six boxes and keep track of your record in each. Over a number of days you can get an excellent idea of your percentages. Try using the same stance (for disguise) from both sides of the court.

Direction (Passing Shots). Perhaps the best way to practice down-the-line passing shots is to rally in the alley with another competent player. Even the most accurate hitters can improve with this drill. Score a point for the other player every time you miss the alley. A variation can be played on the backboard. Draw a chalk line, about two yards from one edge of the board, from as high as you can reach down to the net line. Try to keep a rally going within the space between the line and the edge of the board, counting two points against yourself for missing on the wall side and only one point against for hitting off the board. These drills may help you develop a sort of "tunnel-vision" that can be excellent for concentration.

FOOTWORK — "KAMA-KAZI" DRILLS

Get a friend to help you with these drills, which shouldn't be hard once he sees he'll be torturing you (and that it will only take five minutes). You can increase your speed by running and wind sprints, but you have to be able to hit while you're moving. Thus this peculiar torture:

Side to Side Moving. Your friend starts at net with a bucket of balls and hits the first one wide to your forehand in the backcourt. Just as you are hitting it, he hits another wide to your backhand, and so on, until all the balls have been hit. He will soon find our how fast you are, and he will attempt to make you move a little faster. The same drill can be done with you at net and your friend back.

Up-and-Back Moving. Up-and-back moving is a more universal problem than side-to-side moving. In fact, many players who move quite well to the side seem to be much slower up and back. Sometimes this results from a dislike of the net or because it is hard to anticipate how short a ball will land. Remember that it is better to be earlier than on time, and that bad moving can be overcome. Both Stan Smith and Billie Jean King were slow when they started playing serious tennis. Many fat players have amazed their opponents with their anticipation and seeming ability to cover the court. Have a friend start at the net and hit a short ball. As you are just getting it, he will hit the next one over your head. The first ball does not have to be a drop shot or the next one a lob.

"Shortcourt." Playing an occasional game inside the service lines is valuable practice for one's touch, as there is rarely an opportunity for power. A game must be started with an underhand serve, of course, and played within two or four of the service boxes. Playing in four boxes can be exhausting exercise, while playing in two boxes can lead to long rallies with one player close to the net volleying. As every shot must bounce first in the boxes, even an overhead is apt to be hit carefully.

15

Injuries and Conditioning

Tennis is rigorous exercise and demands superior conditioning. As your timing improves you will be able to hit better shots, but so will your worthy opponents. The intermediate may dream of ending points earlier with better shots, but opponents learn to anticipate more skillfully, and points become harder to win. This natural escalation of activity leads to increasing physical commitments. Some people still think of tennis in terms of its modern origins on the lawns of English lords — as a sport in which anyone can indulge. The game, of course, has become more rigorous, but it is interesting to note that the lordly English have invented some of the most punishing sports in the world (even if they are played with rackets). Squash "rackets" is a strenuous game as we know it in America, but an English squash match can last brutal hours longer. (It is played in a slightly larger court with a softer ball and with different rules for scoring.) Its champions train by running twenty miles a day in soft sand. Another English "game," called "racquets," has been likened to a cross between dodge ball and squash taking place in a driving range with metal walls.

At its most graceful, tennis is still a game of twisting and straining, full of fast sprints and sudden turns. It is said that tennis players complain more about physical impairments than other athletes. "I've never lost to him when I was healthy," is a familiar expression. It is not a sport of broken bones, as are the contact sports. The most common injury spots are elbows and backs, although knees, ankles, shoulders, wrists, and all muscles receive their share of punishment at every level of play. The unmatched excitement of competing in tennis lures everyone to push himself, at times. Among the current troop of international professionals, Billie Jean King, Tom Okker, Cliff Drysdale and Arthur Ashe (to name a few) tennis elbow is a shared complaint. Two-time Forest Hills finalist Tony Roche, the stocky son of an Australian butcher, was forced into a premature semiretirement by a tennis elbow. Now, after almost three years of training, he is trying to re-emerge.

Most tennis injuries are preventable and curable — even tennis elbow. But worrying about them can take some of the enjoyment out of the game. When trying to improve, don't leave conditioning for later. Tennis is more fun without a struggle to bring conditioning up to a level where skills can be enjoyed, though a certain pride should be taken in conditioning for its own sake. The exercises described in this chapter are widely recommended for curing or preventing injuries, as well as for improving overall condition.

Using heavy weights is not suggested, nor is any exercise that could be physically harmful if done improperly by a normal person. Of course, if you have a bad injury you should see a doctor. With the tennis boom, more and more doctors are becoming capable of recommending exercises for ailments. *Start on the light side* of all exercise and build up gradually (muscles can be strained at first). Continuity, not severity, is the wisest policy.

HAND, WRIST AND ELBOW EXERCISES

Slamming a tennis ball over and over with a thirteen ounce racket puts considerable strain on the arm. The shock of this strain is absorbed mostly by the arm from the elbow down. An obvious beginning requirement is the "firm handshake" needed to grip the racket. Few serious injuries are inflicted to hands on the tennis court (sore knuckles can be an irritation after years of play), but a little grip strengthening is a simple matter, and good for the wrists as well. Squeeze a pocket-size device for several minutes a day on the subway or while watching the news. It relieves tension and can become habitual. Finger-tip push-ups are fine for those who can do them. All the exercises listed below for the elbow are beneficial to the wrist and hand.

Anyone who thinks of himself as at least a weekend tennis player can expect some elbow trouble sometime, but moonlighting as a golfer is not necessary. Tennis elbow can, of course, be excruciatingly painful, but everyone's elbow problem is slightly different. The physical basis for elbow pain is fairly well understood by doctors interested in the subject. There are usually two kinds of tennis elbow problems, both involving the two major tendon complexes in the elbow. One complex is affected frequently by backhand strokes, especially those backhands which feature elbow usage (the "poke"). The other complex is a trouble spot for tennis professionals, and I will not attempt to explain the differences in more detail, since the treatment for both problems is similar.

A strained tendon inflames the surrounding area, and the swelling causes pain. "Cold," applied right after playing or otherwise straining, provides the best immediate relief. Before play, if an elbow injury permits you to play (and many do), the elbow will need careful "warming-up." During play an arm brace, wrapped around the arm about an inch or two below the elbow, absorbs some of the shock before it gets to the sore joint (the same principle as a fret on a guitar). Braces are marketed commercially and can be purchased for a dollar or so in almost any sporting goods store with a tennis line.

Should your elbow be terribly painful, with playing out of the question, it may require cortisone shots to reduce the swelling. Acupuncture has recently been tried as emergency treatment.

Ordeals with tennis elbow last for an unpredictable length of time. Some problems nag on without changing for a time, while others disappear as suddenly as they struck (not all tennis elbows "strike"). Cortisone and acupuncture have been known to perform amazing cures, but it is generally accepted that tennis elbows get better with time and *strength*. Whether or not an elbow problem has already developed, the light exercises below are strongly recommended.

Two "tennis" doctors recommended "tennis elbow" exercises of the variety described below in a cover story for a tennis magazine in 1974. Attach a light weight (perhaps a couple of pounds for men, less for women) to the head of an old tennis racket and do the following:

1. Rest the arm straight out on a table, with the racket lying face-down on the surface, at a right angle to the arm. Gripping the racket with a forehand grip, turn wrist and elbow slowly to raise the racket perpendicular to the table. Lower it slowly, rest,

and repeat five or ten times. If it seems a big effort, lessen the weight.

2. Do the same with a backhand grip, bringing the racket up from the other side.

If your elbow is already injured, start by using less weight.

A slightly harder exercise is done by tying a half-pound weight to four feet of string and fastening the other end to the throat of the racket. Gripping the racket with one hand on either side of the string, turn the racket until the weight has been lifted to the racket. Then let it down to the ground again. The arms should be held straight out from the body throughout the exercise.

Push-ups, pull-ups and other exercises involving an elbow bend are probably not good for injured elbows, but they provide good exercise otherwise. Those with elbow problems will have to find other means of strengthening shoulders and upper arms (see below).

UPPER TORSO EXERCISES

Besides push-ups and pull-ups, any isometric pushing will probably strengthen the shoulder and back muscles. For a case in point, push for 10 seconds against a wall with your right hand as if it were the racket face. Stomach and back muscles, as well as arm and shoulder muscles, can be employed. Torn shoulder muscles can receive good training by slowly swinging a weighted racket. There is probably no more exact way of treating tennis muscles in the shoulder and back. The player who wants to add power to his serve should practice daily swinging the weighted racket (though carefully at first).

Back problems occupy a special territory where no layman should dare to trespass. If you have a "bad" back, see a doctor to avoid seriously damaging it playing tennis. While tennis — especially serving — is hard on backs, a strong back will not be affected. The excessive development of one side of the body in tennis players is seldom a problem. Here are a few general comments about back care and training, part of which will probably sound familiar.

Good posture and rest are not to be underestimated in their effect on backs. Tennis players develop tight muscles that need to be loosened up before play, and this applies above all to backs. Start looking for exercises that do the best job loosening you up — the section below on "warming up" describes the exercises most commonly done by tennis players.

Some of the exercises that loosen the back can also be used to strengthen it. Exercises that strengthen the shoulders and stomach muscles are good for the back, as is running.

STOMACH AND LEG EXERCISES

Although the stomach muscles do not seem to partake in any direct action on the tennis court, they must be in shape in order to endure the stress of constant stretching and running. *Leg lifts* are the purest form of stomach exercise. Lie flat on the floor on your back (not after a meal) and slowly raise the legs, together, one foot off the ground. Hold for three seconds, then lower slowly. Repeat several times, and do daily (increasing the holding time every ten days).

Though leg lifts also help the leg muscles, running is the best leg exercise. *Jogging* a comfortable distance is wonderful exercise. If a more demanding leg exercise is desired, *"wind sprints"* can be done. Start sprinting, go five yards, stop and walk five yards, and start again. Continue until exhausted. Wind sprints build the kind of speed a tennis player needs, and they help the "wind" more than running long distances. It is said that during a three-set match of singles, each player will run several miles — most of it sprinting or hopping. *Jumping rope* is suggested for those who can run but are not light on their feet. More rigorous leg exercises are running in soft sand or up and down stairs.

WARMING UP

The short time allowed for a warm-up before a match is barely sufficient to begin familiarizing yourself with an opponent's game, or to do more than perfunctorily warm up your own game. There is definitely not time to bring a body from its normal temperature and condition to a match readiness. Rather than pulling a muscle by trying to start too quickly or resigning yourself to a slow start, get into the habit of *warming up off the court*. Time and space are not always available before a match, and muscles need some warming up before vigorous use. Sore muscles may demand that you begin perspiring before you can play without pain.

A little wind mill stretching (fig. 15 - 1), trunk bending (fig. 15 - 2), toe touching and back rolling are good preliminaries to 50 - 100 jumping jacks, jumping rope, or jogging ("in place" or for one-fifth of a mile). End with a few push-ups (men's or women's) and a few leg lifts.

LOOSENING UP AND RELAXING

Tennis muscles are tight and can be kinky. Most players need to do exercises which will loosen the muscles as well as relax them so that they can be warmed up. Five to fifteen minutes of *yoga* is by far the most soothing and effective loosening up exercise. Below is a series of several elementary yoga exercises which can be done quickly by anybody and embellished in ways that can be discovered or read about. For those who sit at a desk all day, a little yoga done in the morning (or during a break) will ease back and neck tension, loosen tight legs, improve posture and generally increase alertness. While *it will not cause perspiration,* yoga can be the only warming up necessary before walking out on the court. Yoga breathing exercises are not discussed here, though they are very beneficial if particular psyching up or relaxing is necessary (and if time is available).

1. *(One minute) Get your blood circulating* to all parts of the body. When you are inactive, your blood stays in certain areas of your body. Before loosening your muscles, it is absolutely necessary to stretch and get the blood moving. Sit on the floor and quickly massage all the parts of your body that you can reach, starting with the temples, the face, the scalp and the neck, and then move down to the toes.

2. *(Thirty seconds) First stretching exercise.* Still sitting on the floor, stretch one leg straight out in front of your body. Bending the other leg out of the way, lean over from the waist and work to touch your toes (fig. 15 - 3). Do with both legs alternately.

Figure 15-1

Figure 15-2

Figure 15-3

Figure 15-4

3.   (One to two minutes) Second stretching exercise. On a
rug or on the grass, sit on your ankles with your back straight
and your chin up (fig 15 - 4). Hold the position for a while
and then start to lean slowly back, as far as you can comfor-
tably. To loosen your shoulders and upper back, try putting
your fists together behind your neck and pushing them
against each other. To relax, lean forward and rest your
forehead on the floor.

4. (Thirty seconds) Back roll. Lie back on a rug with your legs in the air (figs. 15 - 5A and 15 - 5B). Roll from side to side. Rolling down the length of your spine will put more pressure on the vertebrae, and thus loosen the back more.

Figure 15-5A

Figure 15-5B

5.   *(One to two minutes) Shoulder stand.* (fig 15 - 6). This exercise rushes the blood to your head and puts a constant, mild pressure on all the muscles of the torso. Very good for muscle tone. Do a few slow scissors splits with legs in the air to loosen hamstrings.

Figure 15-6

6. *(Forty-five seconds) The yoga toe touch.* Rather than bending over and lunging for the toes, lean over slowly with your back straight and your chin up (fig. 15-7). When you get as far down as you can with your back straight, relax your posture letting the head and arms dangle for ten seconds. Try, in other words, to reach for the toes by bending from the waist instead of stretching with the arms. To come back up, straighten your back, pull your chin up, put your hands back on your hips and rise slowly back into a standing position. Repeat once or twice. Depending on how loose your lower back is, you should or should not actually touch your toes.

Figure 15-7

These last two exercises are optional, and will strengthen the back and arms as well as stretching them.

7. *Shoulder stand variation.* From the shoulder stand position shown in fig. 15-7, lower your legs over your head. Keeping your knees straight, hold them a foot over your head for ten seconds, and then relax the knees and rest for ten seconds. Continue the pattern for a minute or two. Some people may find it comfortable to rest with their feet on the floor, behind their head.

8. *Yoga push-ups.* The yoga push-up can be easily done by men or women. It is designed to allow a greater range of difficulty than a regular push-up, and to further stretch the back. Lie flat on your stomach with your head resting on your chin, place your hands palm down by your ears, with your elbows pointing out to the side (fig. 15 - 8). Lift your torso slowly from the waist with your back (also "pushing up" with the arms) until your arms are straight; rest, and lower yourself as slowly as you can. Repeat several times or more.

Figure 15-8

Appendix

Selecting a Racket
Wood vs. Metal

For Beginners. Beginners usually pick a racket for reasons of price and durability. Wood and metal rackets of dubious quality and stringing can be bought on "sale" at department stores for under fifteen dollars. It is anyone's guess whether such products will survive normal punishment, but don't buy anything that rattles or is cracked. If you are strong and want a medium or heavy-weighted racket, you will probably be able to get the "feel" faster with a wood racket. Metal rackets are more streamlined and move through the air with so little resistance that it can be difficult to feel your swing. Slight ladies should begin with a metal racket, because they need all the power they can get. Unless you are at either extreme of the strength spectrum, your choice of metal or wood will not be significant. It is more important to select a racket that will last.

For twenty-five dollars a good wood racket (already strung) can be purchased from a reputable sporting goods store where they will often give you a quality restringing job when the time comes. If you take proper care of your racket, the strings should last well over a year and the frame ought to tolerate one or two complete restringings without becoming too weak. Nylon strings are by far the most sensible buy. They are more weather resistant than gut and cost half the price. Gut is only of value in a good frame and if the player has advanced well beyond needing to get a "feel" for the game. Metal rackets last longer than wood, but they cost a few dollars more. Do not spend a lot of money on a racket without consulting an expert concerning its grip size and its proper weight for you.

APPENDIX

For Intermediates. Intermediates who play frequent weekend tennis will get the most for their money and their tennis game if they buy quality rackets and have them professionally strung. Wood frames run from a little over twenty to almost fifty dollars; metal frames run from twenty-five to sixty. An eight- or twelve-dollar nylon stringing job will give you excellent play and durability.

On the average, metal frames last a little longer than current-day wood frames. If you have an old wooden relic from another era, don't expect the new wood frame to last as long. The frames of today are thinner and more responsive, but they can warp quickly if not kept dry in a racket press.

Switching from a wood to a metal racket without good reason is likely to cause problems in your game as it is to solve them, though intermediates should be able to adjust to either type in a matter of time. One definite reason to switch would be to alleviate tennis elbow. Metal rackets absorb more shock on impact with the ball and take some of the strain from the arm; they also feel lighter because they are less wind resistant. If you think you *should* change to metal, discuss it with an expert who knows *your* game and talk to other players of your general style and ability. What is right for one style may not be right for another, and within every style there are advocates of both wood and metal.

Factory-strung rackets should be avoided as the stringing job was probably a loose one to prevent the racket from warping or weakening before it was sold. Every racket weakens under the pressure of the strings, and the strings loosen up with time.

For Advanced Players. When one's *feel* is very advanced, a decision to use a wood or metal racket is more important. As the advanced player will know more specifically how he can improve his game, he will be primarily concerned how the properties of wood and metal will affect various strokes (checking pluses and minuses).

Wood rackets are bulkier — more wind resistant. Although a metal racket can be swung with less effort, it is harder to feel the swing. If control is your problem, not power, then the wood racket is probably best for you.

Wood rackets are the less responsive of the two; some metal rackets are so lively they seem to play for you. This is an advantage if you are over-exerting yourself to get the power you know you can control — if power is your problem rather than control, think about a metal racket.

Advanced players almost inevitably find their service power increases with a metal racket. However, if your serve is not going to be a major weapon, a slight increase in service power will not be worth a sacrifice in the control of your other strokes.

Glossary of Tennis Terms

A

Ace   A winning shot which is not touched by the losers's racket.

"Ad" court   The "backhand court" for a right-handed player.

Advanced player   One who has developed sound ground strokes and a second serve that is neither weak nor inconsistent.

Advantage receiver   Scoring term signifying that the player(s) returning serve have won the "deuce" point and can win the game from the backhand court (vs. advantage server).

Alley   The 4½ foot area on each side of the singles court which makes the court playable for doubles.

"American Twist" serve   An exaggerated topspin serve in which the back is bent to hit the ball a foot behind the head.

Angle   A shot which bounces toward the sidelines.

Angle of the racket face   The tilt of the racket face. Either the top edge of the face will be behind the bottom edge ("open" face), vice-versa ("closed" face), or the face will be perpendicular to the ground.

B

Backboard   Any flat wall which will bounce balls back onto a reasonable playing surface.

Backcourt   All areas nearer to the base line than to the service line.

Backhand   A "ground stroke" that is hit with the racket arm in front of the body and the back of the hand leading the racket.

Backhand court   The side of the court (divided by the center line between the service boxes) on which a right-handed player would normally hit a backhand.

Backspin (underspin)   The turning (spinning) of the ball in flight from top to back to bottom.

Backswing   The preparatory part of any swing that takes the racket away from the direction the stroke will aim the ball.

Base line   The line on either side of the net that runs parallel to the net on the far end of the court.

Beginner   One who has never played before or who has not played enough to develop habits or patterns in the basic swings (forehand, backhand, serve and volley).

C

Cannonball   A hard, flat serve, usually the first serve, with little margin for error.

Center line   The line separating the two service boxes, often reappearing as a stub on the baseline to prevent players from serving to the middle of the court (a foot-fault).

Chip   A low sliced ball of medium speed which is not a drive or a dink.

Chop   See "Cut."

Closed racket face   The tilt of the top edge of the racket face toward the net.

Closed stance   A stance more than ninety degree sideways from the direction the ball is coming.

Crosscourt   A shot that is hit from one side of the court to the side diagonally across the net (for example, from one backhand court to the other backhand court). A crosscourt can travel the longest distance between base lines and pass over the lowest part of the net (the middle 3 feet).

Cut (chop)   A severe slice (often accidental) which removes most of the forward pace of the ball. Except when involved in the production of a drop shot, a cut is a trick shot and serves little function in advanced tennis.

GLOSSARY

D

Davis Cup   Annual invitational men's team competition started in 1900 by Dwight Davis.

Default   To forfeit a match before play is begun or finished.

Depth   Where the ball bounces in the court.

Deuce   40 - 40 in score.

Deuce court   Forehand court of a right-handed player.

Dink   A shot that barely goes over the net and drops before the service line, but is not meant to be a drop shot.

Double fault   Two consecutive service errors (first serve and second serve) that lose the point for the server.

Down-the-line   A shot that is hit from one side of the court to the side straight across the net (for example, from the forehand court to the backhand court).

Drive   A ground stroke that is hit fairly fast and low over the net.

Drop shot   A shot which bounces well within the service boxes (not a serve) and does not bounce much toward the baseline.

E

Error   A shot which does not go over the net or does not bounce within bounds of the singles or doubles court. If your racket touches the ball but you do not return it, you have lost the point on an error rather than an ace. Many errors are forced, of course.

F

Face   See "racket face."

Fault   A service error.

First serve   The first of two chances to begin each point, usually hit with more pace and aimed more exactly.

Follow-through   The part of the swing which takes place after contact with the ball has been made.

Foot fault   A serve which, regardless of its bounce, is called a fault by a base line judge or umpire, becaue the foot crossed or touched the base line or center line (where the stub is) before contact with the ball was made.

Footwork   The moving of the feet during a stroke (and to position oneself between strokes — see positioning).

Forecourt   All areas nearer the service line than the base line.

Forehand   A ground stroke that is hit with the racket arm behind the body.

Forehand court   The side of the court on which a right-handed player would normally hit a forehand.

G

Game   The unit in scoring served entirely by one player.

Get   A difficult return.

Grip   1. The position of the hand(s) on the handle of the racket.
2. The leather or plastic that surrounds the handle.

Ground stroke   Any stroke during a rally made after the ball has bounced on the court surface.

H

Half-volley   A shot that is hit just after the first bounce.

I

Intermediate   One who has developed patterns or habits in the basic swings (forehand, backhand, serve and volley).

L

Lob   A shot that passes at least six or seven feet over the net.

Love   A score of zero in a game, set, or match.

O

Open stance   A stance less than ninety degree sideways from the direction the ball is coming.

Out   A ball that first bounces beyond the court boundary lines.

Overhead (smash)   A stroke that meets a ball over the head during a point (after the serve).

P

Passing shot   A shot that is intended to go beyond the reach of the netman.

Point   Smallest scoring value.

Pling   Hitting with an extremely bent elbow.

Positioning   A player's strategic moving in anticipation of the next shot.

Push   To play with no greater ambition than to return every ball; to wait for the opponent to err or attack.

Pusher   One who pushes.

Put-away   A shot which is easily made a winner by dint of a very easy opportunity.

R

Racket face   The strung plane of the racket.

Racket head   The part of the racket that contains the strings.

Racket throat   The racket shaft between the head and the grip.

Rally   (not to be confused with a volley) An exchange of shots back and forth over the net.

Ready position   The stance taken while waiting for an opponent to hit, when no positioning is necessary (for the return of serve).

S

Second serve   The second of the two chances to begin a point, usually hit less hard than the first.

Serve   The stroke used to begin a point (customarily hit over the head) from behind the base line.

Serve-and-volley   A tactic used, mostly on fast courts and in doubles, in which the serve is followed to net.

Service box (or block)   One of the four rectangular areas on a court whose parameters are a singles' sideline, a service line, a center line, and the net. Only the serve must bounce within a service box.

Service line   The first line running parallel to the net on each side of the net.

Set   A scoring unit, normally over when one side has won six games and is ahead by two games.

Set-up   A slow, high shot which bounces inside a service box provides a player with an easy opportunity to hit down into the court.

Shot   1. Any volley, groundstroke or serve. 2. In advanced jargon, a "shot" sometimes describes a "risky" volley, ground stroke or serve; often a variation on a normal stroke. ("Of all players today, Ilie Nastase is the most incredible *shotmaker*.")

Sidelines   The lines which run from base line to base line and mark off the alleys.

Sidespin   The turning (or spinning) of the ball from side to back to side. Sidespin will make the ball curve in the direction in which it is turning.

Slice   Any spin which is not topspin (a chip, a sidespin, a cut).

Spin   The turning of the ball in its flight, in any direction.

Stance   The position of the feet for a shot.

GLOSSARY

T

Topspin The turning (spinning) of the ball in its flight, from bottom to back to top.

Touch An advanced ability to feel the ball well enough to make effective soft shots and angles.

Trade A rally in which neither player tries to gain much advantage from his opponent.

U

Underspin (see backspin)

V

Volley (not to be confused with a rally) Any shot hit before the first bounce.

W

Waiting position (see ready position)

Wimbledon Largest annual invitational championship (held in Wimbledon, England).

Winner Any shot which is completely unreturnable for an opponent.